JOHN HULBERT was brought up in St Andrews and ~~~ ~~
medicine at the University of Edinburgh. ~
research, he changed direction and worke~
general practitioner. In 1979 he and his wi
moved to the Perthshire village of Longfor;
Gowrie.

In 1995, he was elected to Perth & Kinr
as Provost from 2007 to 2012.

In 2010, Provost Hulbert led Perth's high-profile 800th
anniversary celebrations and then the successful campaign to
recover the ancient dignity of City Status, which had been
unceremoniously removed when local government was
reorganised in 1975.

As Provost, he studied Perth's history and development, and
gained a unique insight into its societies and institutions. He has
visited and photographed all of its important buildings. This
information has been crystallised into the first comprehensive
guide book for modern Perth.

*John Hulbert's guide to Perth is a magnificent combination of historical
analysis and contemporary appreciation of our fine City. It is an invaluable
book, written with such care and precision by a former Provost, who led the
effort to restore Perth to its rightful place as a city of Scotland.*
JOHN SWINNEY

# PERTH

A comprehensive guide
for locals and visitors

John Hulbert

**Luath** Press Limited
EDINBURGH
www.luath.co.uk

First published 2015
Reprinted 2015

ISBN: 978-910021-43-9

The paper used in this book is recyclable. It is made from
low chlorine pulps produced in a low energy, low emissions manner
from renewable forests.

Printed and bound by
The Charlesworth Group, Wakefield

Maps by Mike Fox

All images by John Hulbert except where otherwise stated

Typeset in 8.5 point Sabon by
3btype.com

*For Sara*

# Contents

| | | |
|---|---|---|
| MAP 1 | Perth City Centre | 8 |
| MAP 2 | Perth and its Surrounding Area | 10 |
| | Acknowledgements | 13 |
| | Foreword, by Mark Webster, Former Chairman of the Gannochy Trust | 15 |
| | Preface | 17 |
| CHAPTER ONE | Introduction | 19 |
| CHAPTER TWO | The Lade, City Wall and Castle: Perth's Mediaeval Defences | 30 |
| CHAPTER THREE | Perth's Bridges | 36 |
| CHAPTER FOUR | Perth's Flood Defences | 40 |
| CHAPTER FIVE | Whisky and Perth | 48 |
| CHAPTER SIX | Perth's Earliest Streets | 55 |
| CHAPTER SEVEN | The Commercial Heart of Perth | 63 |
| CHAPTER EIGHT | The City Centre | 81 |
| CHAPTER NINE | George Street and Tay Street | 100 |
| CHAPTER TEN | Mill Street and Perth's Cultural Quarter | 111 |
| CHAPTER ELEVEN | Perth's Georgian New Town | 123 |
| CHAPTER TWELVE | 'Twixt City Wall and Railway | 136 |
| CHAPTER THIRTEEN | East of the Tay | 148 |
| CHAPTER FOURTEEN | Perth's Parks and Green Spaces | 164 |
| CHAPTER FIFTEEN | Perth's Suburban Arc | 185 |
| CHAPTER SIXTEEN | Sir Walter Scott and the Fair Maid of Perth | 196 |
| CHAPTER SEVENTEEN | Shopping in Perth | 200 |
| CHAPTER EIGHTEEN | Perth's War Memorials | 204 |
| CHAPTER NINETEEN | Civic Perth | 212 |
| | Index | 221 |

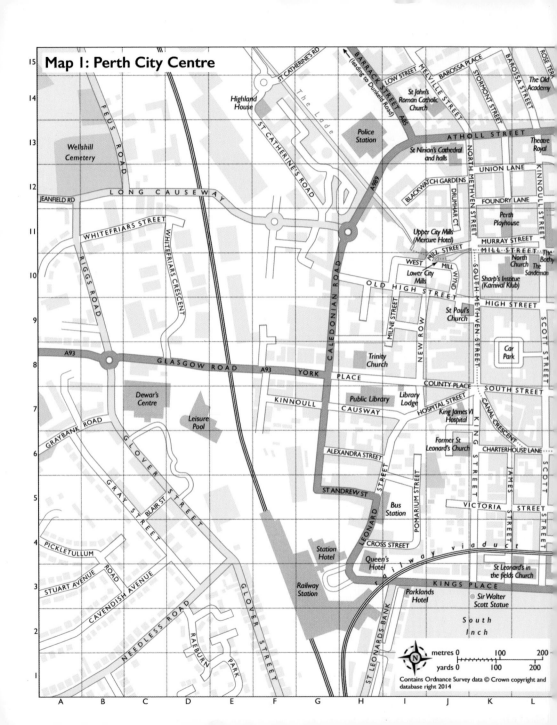

# Map 1: Perth City Centre

Contains Ordnance Survey data © Crown copyright and database right 2014

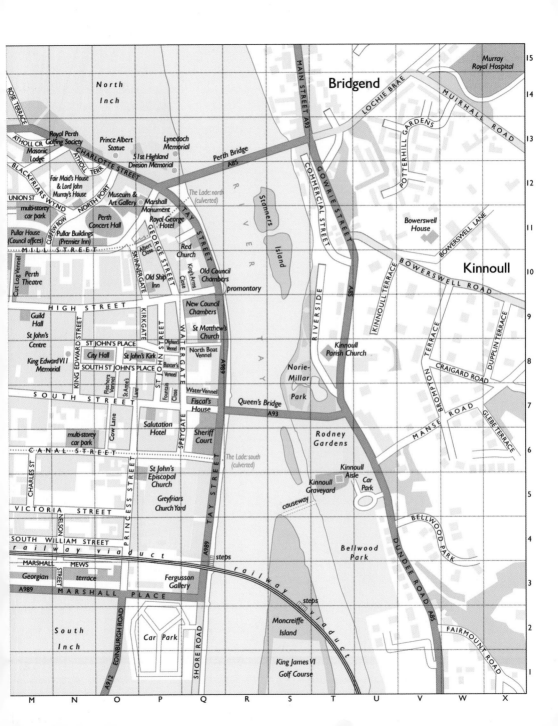

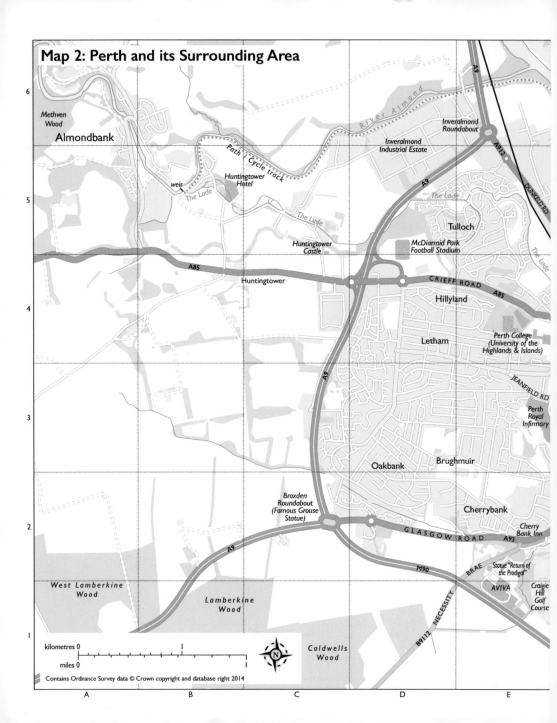

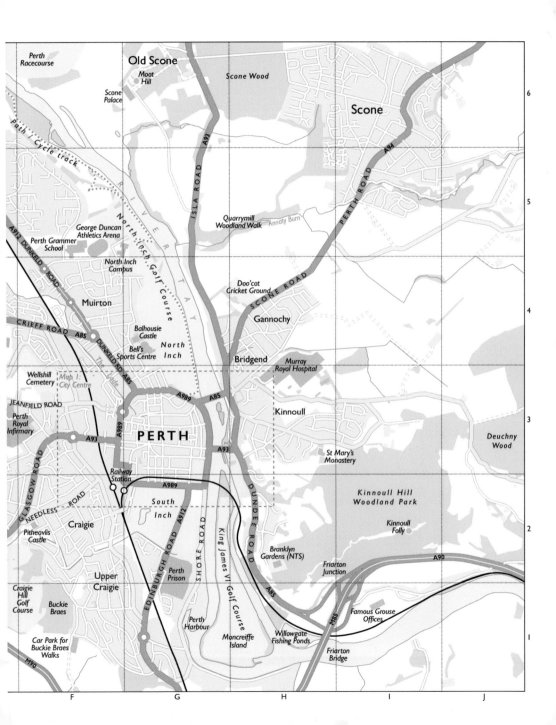

# Acknowledgements

During my time as Provost of Perth & Kinross, it became increasingly clear to me that there was no appropriate guide book for the town, now the City, of Perth. However, the idea of writing the book myself was crystallised during a meeting with Mark Webster, then the Chairman of the Gannochy Trust, and Stewart McLeod, then the Moderator of the Society of High Constables of Perth. They were concerned that the generality of the citizens of Perth, and in particular the younger generation, knew very little about the buildings, streets, and significant features of their home town. At that meeting we discussed ways to address this problem, and while a book like this was not mentioned, it is appropriate for me to thank them now for the inspiration.

During the years spent writing this book and taking the photographs, I have received help from many people. Particular thanks, however, are due to David Strachan and Andrew Driver, of the Perth & Kinross Heritage Trust, to Steve Connelly, the Council's archivist, and to the staff of the Perth Museum and Art Gallery. My thanks are also due to Doug Pringle, the Church officer of St John's Kirk; to Ian Cassells, the Kirk's carillonneur; Russell Logan, of the Lodge Scoon and Perth No. 3 Masonic lodge; and James Mackenzie, the Hospital Master of the King James VI Hospital all of whom were of great assistance.

I owe a debt to Paul Phillipou, Jeremy Duncan, and Rhoda Fothergill who read and commented on all of the text, and to Andrew Driver and Marjory Howatt who read the sections relevant to their particular knowledge. I am particularly grateful to Mark Webster for his comments on AK Bell and the Gannochny Trust, and for writing the Foreword. I expect that there may still be some omissions and inaccuracies, but these are entirely my responsibility.

Above all, however, my thanks are due to my dear wife, Sara, who has supported me unfailingly in the endeavour. She made intuitive suggestions about the text, cast an artistic eye on all the photographs, and has been a meticulous proof reader. It is with great gratitude that I dedicate the book to her.

# Foreword

## by Mark Webster, Former Chairman of the Gannochy Trust

How over five centuries ago could the game of tennis play a significant part in Perth's history? Read this book and you will discover how that happened and on the way you will also discover many other facets of the city's fascinating history as well as a wealth of information about life in Perth today.

John Hulbert's opinions of the public art around the city will surely encourage many, particularly locals, to look afresh at several items to see if they agree with his views. For potential visitors to Perth this book benefits from many carefully chosen photographs, most of which have been taken by the author. Not only do these well illustrate the text but the passion with which they are presented will surely encourage the reader to view firsthand what he describes.

From the time John Hulbert moved with his family to Perthshire more than thirty years ago he has immersed himself in the life of the area which led him to seek and attain election to Perth & Kinross Council in 1995. His love of Perth and its people combined with his acquired knowledge of the city's rich history gained specific momentum when he was elected Perth's Provost in 2007. First of all he led the celebrations to mark the 800th Anniversary of the grant of the city's Royal Charter and used these celebrations to launch the campaign to regain official recognition of Perth as a city. Previous opportunities to bid for official status had not been taken; there had been complacency: local people had always regarded Perth as a city and there was insufficient appreciation of the benefits of obtaining recognition.

John Hulbert fully understood the importance of regaining city status but importantly also knew the overwhelming historical entitlement of Perth to that status. He took up the challenge with vigour and masterminded the campaign; he used every available opportunity to pursue this aim. His extended term as Provost gave him just enough time to achieve the prize of regaining city status before his time in office ended.

John Hulbert is well qualified to unlock the tennis mystery and to explain why Perth is indeed the Fair City.

# Preface

The purpose of this book is to give local citizens and visitors a comprehensive, well-illustrated guide to the City of Perth. It seeks to describe the main features of the city, its buildings, streets and its most important characters, setting them in their historical and cultural context.

The guide is in three parts. Chapters 1–5 give an overview of Perth's development as Scotland's capital, and only walled and moated city. The Lade, the city wall, Perth's bridges and the regular flooding by the river, were all vital elements in that development, as was its hub position in Scotland at the first bridging point on the River Tay, and gateway to the Highlands.

The whisky industry was hugely important to Perth's development in the 20th century. Although it employs few people now, its legacy still influences the city's development.

Chapters 6–15 deal with the various areas of Perth. The section starts with Perth's remaining mediaeval streets close to the site of the original harbour, the source of its wealth and influence. It continues to

The public face of Perth: Tay Street from the east bank.

1 *Perth and Kinross* by John Gifford. 'The Buildings of Scotland' series. Yale University Press, 2007. p. 61.

describe each of the geographical sections of the city separately.

Chapters 16–18 deal with more general matters. These include the importance of the legacy of Sir Walter Scott, the café culture, shopping and the 'Bloom' competitions to Perth's tourist success. Mention is made of Perth's iconic war memorials, and its achievement in becoming Scotland's first *Cittaslow* town and the recovery of City Status. Public art is important in every community to reflect its values and stimulate its creativity. John Gifford in the *Perth and Kinross* volume in the 'Buildings of Scotland' series states: 'Public

sculpture of the late 20th and early 21st centuries has been commissioned in pleasing quantity and quality.'[1] The book includes a photographic record of this art.

Finally, in Chapter 19, the visitor is introduced to some of Perth's important traditions and institutions.

It is impossible, and would be undesirable, to mention all the shops, hotels, cafés, restaurants and churches in a book such as this. Individual buildings are mentioned if they are of particular interest, contribute significantly to the townscape, or if what goes on in the building is of importance to Perth.

The promontory, jutting out from the Tay Street floodwall, at the foot of the High Street.
MAP 1 · Q8

# Introduction

Welcome to Perth, the heart of Scotland.

For the visitor wishing to understand Perth, its history, its buildings, and its place in modern Scotland, the starting place should be 'the promontory' on Tay Street, at the foot of the High Street.

From this balcony, built out over the Tay from the flood defence wall, the High Street stretches westwards in a gentle curve, as it has done for 1,000 years, while behind you, there is a fine view of the river and its bridges. It is an excellent vantage point from which to absorb Perth's origins and development.

## Ancient History

People have inhabited the banks of the Tay for several millennia. In 2001 a late Bronze Age log boat, which had lain undisturbed in the silt of the Tay for 3,000 years, resurfaced some five miles downstream from Perth. In an extremely delicate operation, it was recovered and has been conserved. It is the second oldest log boat in Scotland, and one of the best preserved in the UK.

The origin of the name 'Perth' is likely to be a Pictish survival into the Gaelic era. It is related to the Old Welsh word 'Pert', meaning a wood or copse, which probably existed on the flood free mound in the centre of the town on which St John's Kirk now stands.

## River Tay

The Tay is by far the largest river (by volume of water) in the United Kingdom and is Perth's *raison d'être*. Perth was at the first bridging and fording point of the river, and from Perth, Scotland's early road network fanned out to all points of the compass. Just north of Perth, the line of the Highland Fault is breached by the Tay valley, providing access to the heart of the Highlands and routes to the north-west and the far north. Perth's situation at the 'Gateway to the Highlands' has been an important element in its historical and cultural development. This is captured symbolically in the sculpture of a heart on one of the pillars on the floodwall. A heart is superimposed on a background which represents the texture of the geography of Scotland. The 'Highland Line' divides the background. To the left (upstream) that texture is rough, signifying the Highlands, while downstream it is smooth.

*Top*:
Smeatons Bridge from above.
MAP 1 · Q12

*Above*:
The Carpow Log Boat.
© David Strachan, Perth
& Kinross Heritage Trust.

Tay Street Pillar.
Perth, the heart of Scotland.

19

*Elcho Castle on the River Tay,*
*by James Hill Cranstoun,*
*1870.*
Courtesy of Malcolm Innes.

Whenever the Duke of Atholl wished to travel from his home at Blair Castle, north of Pitlochry, to Edinburgh, he and his retinue (for he would not be travelling alone), first rode the 35 miles to Perth on horseback. Then, after waiting sometimes for several days for favourable winds and tides, he took a ship down the river to Dundee, and then round the coast of Fife to Leith, and finally a carriage to Edinburgh. The journey could easily take two weeks or more.

Perth's harbour, now downstream from the railway bridge, was, and still is, accessible for sea-going ships. At a time when roads were primitive and dangerous, and nearly all trade was carried by ships, the advantages of a port 30 miles inland were huge. The harbour became one of the busiest, and Perth one of the wealthiest towns in Scotland, with many sea-going ships built in, and crewed from Perth. Now, in the 21st century, Perth is still at the centre of Scotland's transport network – trunk roads and railways, rather than drove roads, river and sea.

Full rigged ship on the headstone of Captain Paddy Readd in Greyfriars graveyard.

# Perth's Place in Scottish History

In 843 AD, Kenneth MacAlpin united the two main competing kingdoms of mainland Scotland to establish the first nation state in Europe and become the first King of Scots (see Chapter 13). For the next 600 years, Perth was *de facto* the capital of Scotland. It was where coronations took place, where the King lived and international treaties were negotiated and signed, and where Scotland's Parliaments and Church Councils were convened.

In about 1127 Perth was one of the first five burghs or towns in Scotland to be created Royal Burghs (the ancient Scottish equivalent of City Status) by King David I. The others were Edinburgh, Stirling, Berwick-upon-Tweed, (now in England), and Roxburgh, which has now almost completely vanished from the map. All of these Royal Charters are now lost. In 1210 King William I, 'The Lion', granted

Perth a second Royal Charter, in gratitude to its citizens for saving his life in the terrible flood of 1209. This Charter is on view in the Perth Museum and Art Gallery.

Perth's pre-eminence lasted for 600 years, until in 1437 King James I was murdered in Blackfriars Monastery in Perth. Thereafter the Royal Court decamped to Edinburgh, which then became Scotland's capital city. Nevertheless, Perth was still the official 'Second City of Scotland', a status it retained until it was arbitrarily demoted to a 'town' in 1975. In 2012 there was much rejoicing across all of Scotland when official City Status for Perth was regained in the Queen's Diamond Jubilee Honours competition. The Letters Patent, signed by the Queen, with the Royal Seal appended, can also be seen in the Museum and Art Gallery.

During the 17th and 18th centuries, Perth's port – the source of its wealth – declined in significance as ships became larger, and therefore less able to negotiate the sandbanks of the Tay. Nevertheless, as a frequent host for the Royal Court and the Scottish Parliament, Perth was still a very important Royal Burgh. With four wealthy monastic establishments in the town, it was also a major religious centre, but one that suffered badly during the Scottish Reformation. This was ignited in Perth in 1559 by the fiery sermon preached by John Knox from the pulpit of St John's Kirk.

The loss of Royal patronage following the Union of the Crowns in 1603, crop failures, the disaster of the Darien Scheme, the Union of the Parliaments in 1707 and the bloody aftermath of the 1745 Uprising all plunged Scotland into recession. However, Perth weathered the economic storms better than many places and before the end of the 18th century, it was ready for a period of rapid expansion, fuelled from 1845 onwards by the coming of the railway. As well as having a strong agricultural base, Perth developed a number of prosperous industries, notably the manufacture of glass, ink, rope and linen, as well as dry cleaning and dying, printing,

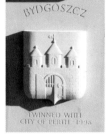

Marshall Place, Georgian terrace overlooking the South Inch.
MAP 1 · N3

Tay Street Pillar.
The Mayor of Cognac, with his wife, the Provost and Lady Provost of Perth, and Gillian Forbes, the sculptor, at the unveiling of the Cognac plaque in 2010.
© Angus Findlay Photography.

brewing, insurance and the blending and bottling of whisky.

Perth grew rapidly at this time, with elegant Georgian streets in the style of the New Town in Edinburgh, and the development of some notable civic buildings. Although the importance of the railways declined after the Second World War, the design of the trunk road network confirmed Perth's hub position in Scotland.

## Continuing European and International Links

Perth's geography and history have combined to mould its culture. In the Middle Ages, its citizens comprised Gaels from the north and Scots-speaking Lowlanders, enriched by a cosmopolitan mix of traders and entrepreneurs from all over northern Europe. These European links

*Top left*:
Tay Street Pillar.
Coat of arms of the city of Aschaffenburg in Bavaria, which was twinned with the City of Perth in 1956.

*Above right*:
Tay Street Pillar.
The Coat of Arms of the City of Pskov in north-west Russia, twinned with Perth in 1991.

*Above left*:
Tay Street Pillar.
Coat of arms of the City of Bydgoszcz, central Poland, twinned with Perth in 1998.

continue and are reflected in Perth's current twinning relationships with cities in Germany, France, north-west Russia and Poland. They are complemented by newer links with Canada, Australia and China.

The Black Watch window in the North Aisle of St John's Kirk.

## Cosmopolitan Royal Burgh with Military Connections

In the past Perth has been an important military town, with particular connections to the Black Watch regiment, which was first raised in 1739 in Aberfeldy. The Black Watch Museum, very recently extended and refurbished, is housed in Balhousie Castle, adjacent to the North Inch. The connection between the city and the regiment is celebrated in a stained glass window in St John's Kirk. This is dedicated to the Sixth Battalion of the Black Watch, which served with such distinction in France in the First World War that the

The Black Watch march past the saluting dais in July 2010 on Perth's 800th anniversary. © Perthshire Picture Agency.

Detail from the Black Watch window. The regimental badge is on the left, with the French *Croix de Guerre* opposite.

*Below left:*

Prince Charles visits the Cairn O'Mhor fruit wine stall at the Perthshire Farmers' market.
© Angus Findlay Photography.

*Below right:*

Perth Theatre entrance.
MAP 1 · M9

French President awarded the Battalion the *Croix de Guerre*. It is a two light window with two Black Watch soldiers, one in ceremonial uniform and the other in battle dress. Behind the first is St Michael with a spear slaying the serpent of evil, and behind the other is St Andrew, the Patron Saint of Scotland. The Regimental badge and the French *Croix de Guerre* feature in the lower part of the window.

Links with the Royal Family are also very important. The late Queen Elizabeth, the Queen Mother, the Duke of York (later George VI) and most recently Prince Philip, Duke of Edinburgh, have all been granted the Freedom of Perth. Prince Charles, as Colonel in Chief of the Black Watch, and the Princess Royal, patron of the Royal Scottish Geographical Society, are frequent visitors.

## Cultural and Sporting Centre

Perth's hub position probably underlies its success as a cultural and sporting centre. The climax of the very crowded cultural calendar is the Perth Festival of the Arts, a ten-day extravaganza of music, theatre and art. It brings large numbers of visitors to Perth at the end of May. Perth's new Concert Hall (opened in 2005) and the late Victorian Perth Theatre (temporarily closed for extensive refurbishment) provide the venues for most of the main events in the Festival. However, Perth also has two magnificent church buildings (the High Kirk of St John, and St Ninian's Cathedral), and many smaller halls, which ensure that there are locations to suit all kinds of performances.

Perth is well endowed with museums. The collection in Perth Museum and Art Gallery was the first in any Local Authority to be designated 'A Recognised Collection of National Significance'. In addition,

Perth has three unique institutions: the Fergusson Art Gallery, dedicated to the Scottish Colourist, JD Fergusson and his lifelong partner Margaret Morris; the Balhousie Castle Museum, which displays 250 years' worth of Black Watch history, records and memorabilia; and the extensive archive of maps, documents and artefacts now housed at the newly established headquarters of the Royal Scottish Geographical Society in the Fair Maid's House and the adjoining Lord John Murray's House.

A broad variety of sporting events attracting international entries take place in Perth every year. Curling is perhaps the most important, but volleyball, bowling (indoor and outdoor), badminton, golf, cycling, orienteering and canoeing all bring competitors and spectators to the area.

Perth is a small but ambitious and prosperous city, with low unemployment and a significant proportion of self-employment. Its main industry is tourism, but it is

*Top left:*

Perth Museum and Art Gallery, and the Old Post Office.
MAP 1 · O12

*Top right:*

Perth Concert Hall at night.
© Jeff Condliffe.
MAP 1 · O11

*Above left:*

The Fergusson Gallery.
MAP 1 · Q3

*Above right:*

Balhousie Castle from the North Inch.
MAP 2 · G4

*Below left:*

The Fair Maid's House and Lord John Murray's House with the arched windows behind.
MAP 1 · N12

The Tay Descent in 2011. Canoes race down the last few yards to the finishing line at the Queen's Bridge.
© Angus Findlay Photography.

home to the head quarters of several large international companies, including Scottish & Southern Energy, Stagecoach, and Highland Spring. Perth is an important Scottish centre for health and education, with two major hospitals (linked to the Dundee University Medical School), the largest campus of the University of the Highlands and Islands, and the headquarters of the Royal Scottish Geographical Society.

Perth is the administrative, retail and commercial centre for a wide area, comprising a large dispersed rural population, many villages large and small, and half a dozen towns. Most notable of these are Pitlochry and Aberfeldy in Highland Perthshire; Crieff, at the head of Strathearn; Auchterarder, on the outskirts of which is Scotland's most famous hotel, Gleneagles; Kinross, on the shores of Loch Leven, the ancient capital of Kinross-shire; and Blairgowrie in East Perthshire, the centre of the soft fruit industry.

## Overview of Perth City

Standing on the promontory on Tay Street and turning one's back on the river, the City of Perth lies before you, its mediaeval street pattern still recognisable in the 21st century. However, in the immediate prospect, the buildings fronting Tay Street are late 19th century, and the floodwall, incorporating the promontory, was completed in 2001, to protect Perth

**The Tay Descent**, a canoe race from Dunkeld down the river to Perth, regularly brings over 400 participants from all over the UK and beyond to the Tay during the fourth weekend of October.

The slogan used in Perth to attract visitors to the many events in the city is 'Ninety minutes' travelling time from 90 per cent of the population of Scotland'.

Perth from the Air. The mediaeval street pattern is still recognisable. © Perth & Kinross Heritage Trust.

*Below*:
Fleshers Vennel runs between South Street and St John's Place.

from the devastating inundations, which are a major feature of its history.

Perth's city centre is remarkably compact, and still mostly contained within the line of the old city walls. In the middle, on a slightly raised mound which, it is said, has never been flooded, is the High Kirk of St John the Baptist. This building, the oldest and most important in Perth, was already a significant building by the 11th century, and has been altered or modified in every century since.

From the Kirk and the square in front of it, the streets of Perth spread out in a tight grid pattern. The main thoroughfares, High Street and South Street, lead from the river westwards to the city wall. Among street names in Scottish towns and cities, the word 'port' refers to a gate, usually in the city wall, whereas the word 'gait', sometimes spelled 'gate', means a

road or thoroughfare. The main streets are still interconnected by a network of narrow lanes, the names of which are all mediaeval in origin, and many give an indication of the trades carried out in that part of the

### Ancient Street Names

Among Perth's old street names are Cow Vennel, Fleshers Vennel, Cut Log Vennel, Skinnergate, Meal Vennel, Horners Lane, and Ropemakers Close. Baxters Vennel (baxter is the old Scots word for baker) where the headquarters of the Baxter Incorporation was

located, was one of the 'Kirk Vennels' linking the Watergate to the Kirk precinct.

Oliphants Vennel, adjacent to Baxters Vennel is so called because the prestigious home of the Oliphant family, who were prominent Jacobites, stood nearby. A notable member of the Oliphant family was Lady Carolina Oliphant, later Lady Nairn, the author of many Jacobite and other Scots songs, such as 'Will ye no come back again', and 'The Laird of Cockpen'.

old city. Such a lane, if it is open to the sky, and connects streets at either end, is called a 'vennel'. If, however, it pierces a building and leads to a courtyard beyond, it is called a 'close' if it is narrow, but a 'pend' if it is wide enough to take a vehicle.

Perth's important buildings and its specialist shops are almost all readily accessible on foot from the promontory, as well as from the railway station, bus terminal and the major car parks in the city.

Perth is well endowed with parkland. To the north and south, close to the city centre and adjacent to the river, lie the Inches – large parks given to the people of Perth by King Robert III in 1377. A condition of the gift was that he should be buried in St John's Kirk. It was said at the time that he 'exchanged two Inches for six feet'. Ultimately, however, it was a futile condition, for he was buried in Paisley Abbey.

Moncreiffe Island in the centre of the river is a large and important area of green space in the centre of Perth, which can be reached by a walkway on the railway bridge from both banks of the Tay. Although prone to flooding, it has an important golf course, numerous allotments and a wild area much used by walkers.

Across the river, on the east bank, are Norie-Miller Park, Rodney Gardens and Bellwood Park, which together form a strip of parkland embellished by many items of modern public art. Beyond that, a network of way-marked paths leads to Kinnoull Hill with its forbidding

The Island Golf Course on Moncreiffe Island. The South Inch lies opposite the tip of the island.

cliffs and picturesque folly. To the west, another series of paths leads past Perth's quarry and the Craigie Golf Course to Mailer Hill. From each of these vantage points, panoramic views of the city and its surroundings reveal how the glaciers of the last ice age gouged a channel through the hills to the south of Perth, enabling the Tay to reach its estuary, and eventually the North Sea.

The mediaeval constraints of the city walls survived almost unchanged until the 18th century, when the line was breached to the west and north. However, it was not until the 19th century, with the coming of the railway, that major expansion took place.

The Folly on Kinnoull Hill in autumn.
MAP 2 · 12

The open prospect of the Inches is jealously guarded by the people of Perth. In the mid-1840s, when the railways came to Perth, it was proposed to build the station on the South Inch, and this found favour with the city fathers. However, there was such a public outcry that the site was moved to its present location, at the south-west corner of the city centre.

# CHAPTER TWO

# The Lade, City Wall and Castle: Perth's Mediaeval Defences

Modern Perth's mediaeval origins are best understood by studying David Simon's imaginative painting of an 'aerial view' of Perth on 12 May 1559. Why the very particular date? Because the image purports to show Perth on the morning after John Knox preached his sermon in St John's Kirk on the 11th of May of that year, and lit the fuse of the Reformation in Scotland. The streets are filled with the 'rascally mob' (as described by John Knox himself) and various religious establishments are shown to be burning. Much detailed research was devoted to ensure the historical and architectural integrity of the buildings shown, their location on the map, and to the overall layout of Perth.

The painting shows a town surrounded by water and a defensive wall. The Lade is a unique feature, hugely important defensively in times of war or siege, vital for the commercial health of

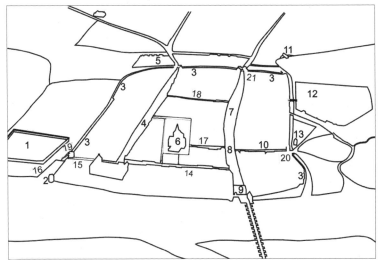

**Legend for David Simon's Map**

1. Franciscan (Greyfriars) Friary
2. Monk's Tower
3. Lade and City wall
4. South Street
5. Carthusian Friary
6. St John's Kirk
7. High Street
8. Market Cross
9. Tolbooth
10. Skinnergate
11. City Mills
12. Dominican Friary
13. St Lawrence Chapel
14. Watergate
15. Speygate
16. Greyfriars Harbour
17. Kirkgate
18. Meal Vennel
19. Spey tower
20. Red Brig Port
21. Turret Port

the town for nearly a thousand years, and now increasingly valued as a wildlife corridor and tourist asset.

## The Town Lade

The Lade arises at Low's Work, a mediaeval weir on the River Almond near Huntingtower Hotel, about four and a half miles north-west of Perth. Low's Work is a B-listed construction, 80 yards long and built in the 11th century with unmortared stone. Severe floods in recent years breached the weir, but Perth & Kinross Council has now repaired it, refurbished the sluice gate, and installed a fish pass.

The Lade is a substantial watercourse, arising from a large river, and supplemented by small streams and field drains throughout its length. It flows east through the village of Ruthvenfield, passes under the A9 just north of the A85 interchange, through the outskirts of Perth, crosses under the railway, and eventually under Perth's inner ring road, near St Ninian's Cathedral. As it nears the City Mills the channel is around 25 feet wide and the water two feet deep and fast flowing. From mediaeval times right up to the early 20th century, the Lade supplied water

The source of the Lade at the weir at Low's Work.
MAP 2 · B5

The Lade, overlooked by modern housing as it approaches the City Mills.
MAP 1 · I11

city, and is now Canal Street. Up until the 19th century the canal dock, or Greyfriars Quay, was an important part of Perth Harbour, with boat-building yards and other marine industries along its bank.

In mediaeval times, the Lade around the city was deep and wide, filling to the brim at high tide and flowing rapidly when the tide ebbed. It was in effect a moat so that, with the River Tay, Perth was completely surrounded by water.

## The Lade as a Modern Tourist Attraction

There is a footpath along the side of the Lade. This is best reached from St Catherine's retail car park just past the Police Station on the Dunkeld Road. The route is flat, (apart from a steep climb up and down over a railway foot bridge), and more like a canal towpath than a river walk. It passes round some modern housing

to mills, bleachfields and other industries along its length.

After it leaves the Lower City Mills, the Lade plunges out of sight beneath Methven Street and divides into two. The northern arm passes along the northern boundary of the mediaeval town, and is now channelled in a culvert under Mill Street. It can still be seen deep below the Red Brig among a series of floodgates and a parapet of red sandstone. It then runs beside what may be the only surviving part of the old city wall, at Albert Close, before diving under George Street to reach the Tay.

The route of the southern arm was along the western boundary of the town, where it still runs in a culvert under Methven Street. It opened into Perth's canal – an artificial arm of the River Tay, which formed the southern boundary of the

The Lade near the Crieff Road.

schemes and an industrial area that is being redeveloped, but much of it is lightly wooded, and there is an abundance of wildlife, including kingfishers. Eventually the Lade disappears into a culvert under the A9. Perth & Kinross Council is developing the route as a wild life corridor.

The source of the Lade is best found by cycling or walking the six miles of the Round Perth Cycle Track, beginning at the dry arch under the Perth Bridge (see map, Chapter 13). This easy, flat route skirts the North Inch, following the bank of the Tay to the confluence with the River Almond. It provides excellent views of the river – in places smooth and deep, elsewhere fast flowing and dangerous. In the middle distance is Scone Palace, and to the north are the Grampian Mountains.

The path then follows the River Almond to the Low's Work Weir near the village of Almondbank. The scenery along the Almond is quite different, with steep wooded banks and much evidence of erosion. Both rivers are, of course, important salmon rivers, and so at the right season there will often be fishermen wading in the river or fishing from boats.

From the weir the Lade passes through the garden of Huntingtower Hotel, where it is possible to have lunch or a drink in the bar, It then winds on through the picturesque Ruthvenfield village, until the culvert under the A9 blocks further progress. Cyclists may return to Perth along the Crieff Road, while for walkers there

is public transport back to Perth from the village of Almondbank.

## The City Wall

The City Wall was built on the inner bank of the Lade, and by the early 14th century had substantial fortifications. John Barbour stated that Perth's walls 'were all of stone with thick walled high-standing towers'[1] to defend it against assault.

1   *The Bruce* by John Barbour. Translated by AAM Duncan, Canongate Classics, 1997, pp. 334–5.

*Top:*
The River Almond, fast flowing between steep, wooded banks.
MAP 2 · B5

The Lade passes through the garden of Huntingtower Hotel.
MAP 2 · B5

## Perth Recaptured by Robert the Bruce

Following the murder of the Red Comyn in Dumfries, Robert the Bruce was crowned King of Scots at Scone on Palm Sunday in March 1306 (see Chapter 11). On 19 June, however, his army was routed by the English at the battle of Methven, about seven miles west of Perth, and he became a fugitive. Perth was in English hands and they strengthened its defences and established a formidable garrison. With its moat and wall, and the ability to bring in supplies by sea and river, Perth was almost impregnable.

Over the next few years, however, Bruce's fortunes gradually improved, as he brought more and more of Scotland under his banner. Perth, however, guarding the routes to the north and north-east remained in enemy hands. In late 1311 Bruce mounted a siege of the town for two months, but with no success. Secure in their defences, and with no shortage of supplies, the English soldiers jeered at Bruce from the parapets of the city walls.

Bruce's response, having surveyed the walls and the Lade, and discovered the places where the defences were most vulnerable, was to march his army away. Two weeks later he returned on a dark night, with a select band of followers. They waded through the Lade, up to their necks in freezing water, carrying spears and ladders. They climbed the walls, surprised the guards and took the town. Soon afterwards the castles of Roxburgh, Dumfries and Edinburgh fell to the Scottish forces. This important event in Perth's history is illustrated in the great east window of Perth's Old City Chambers.

The Great East Window of the Council Chambers. The legend in the north and south panels reads: 'King Robert the Bruce achieved the Freedom of Perth... By scaling the walls and defeating the English garrison in 1311'. Beneath the central window is the name of the donor, 'John Pullar, Lord Provost of Perth, 1867-1873'.

After Bannockburn in 1314, there was a period of reasonable stability until Bruce's death in 1329. He was succeeded by his five-year-old son, David II, who was already married to the daughter of Edward II of England. At the age of seven, in 1331, he was crowned at Scone. Meanwhile Edward Balliol, son of John Balliol, Robert Bruce's predecessor and rival, whom Edward I of England had defeated in 1296, allied himself with England and tried to secure Scotland's throne. With English help he invaded Scotland and defeated the Scottish army at Dupplin Moor just south of Perth. Perth fell without resistance, and Edward Balliol was crowned at

Scone in September 1332. Scotland now had two crowned kings.

During this occupation, the English rebuilt Perth's city wall, including a tower where the southern stretch of the wall reached the Tay. This was called 'The Monk's Tower', probably because of its proximity to the Franciscan Friary. Any traces of this building were lost when Tay Street was built, but its site is marked by one of the pillars in the Tay Street floodwall. The inscription on the pillar is: 'Site of the Monk's Tower at the south-east corner of the city wall. Built about 1336 when Edward III of England refortified the town.'

This tower is also associated with General Monk. Cromwell invaded Scotland in 1651; following his victory at Inverkeithing, he marched on Perth. It is recorded that a reasonably amicable settlement was reached and the gates of the town were opened by Lord Provost Andrew Grant. General Monk was left in charge, and built the huge Citadel on the South Inch (see Chapter 13), and strengthened the city walls, including Monk's Tower.

## The Castle

Perth's castle was a relatively short-lived structure. It was an important feature of Perth's defences in the early 1100s, and is mentioned in a charter of King Malcolm IV, when it was used as a fortified base and served as the centre of the royal administration. It was built just outside the city wall, probably on a raised mound near to where the Perth Museum now stands. It stood guard over the mediaeval bridge and routes to the north and north-east. There is a representation of the castle on a bronze plaque on the 'dry' side of the floodwall at the North Inch Memorial Garden. It shows a wooden keep on a large mound. Below it, within a defensive palisade are houses, and on the left the mediaeval bridge.

The castle was certainly occupied by King William the Lion on a stormy day in 1209, when Perth suffered one of its most severe floods. The castle and the mediaeval bridge were swept away, and the King's life saved only by the actions of some brave Perth citizens. The castle was never rebuilt, but the King expressed his gratitude to the people of Perth the following year by renewing Perth's Royal Charter, which had first been granted by King David I in around 1127 (see Chapter 1).

Tay Street Pillar on the site of the Monk's Tower at the south-east corner of the city wall.

Bronze plaque, adjacent to the North Inch floodgate showing Perth Castle and the mediaeval bridge. MAP 1 · P12

Artist's impression of the appearance of the castle, city wall and the mediaeval bridge. © Perth Museum & Art Gallery, Perth & Kinross Council.

# Perth's Bridges

As the River Tay is Perth's *raison d'être*, so Perth's bridges have been essential for its commercial success from mediaeval times to the present. For hundreds of years there was just one bridge (or no bridge at all), and that bridge was called the Perth Bridge.

## The Perth Bridge

The current Perth Bridge, a graceful structure of great strength, is one of the most recognisable features of Perth, and is an icon for the city. Designed by John Smeaton of Eddystone Lighthouse fame, and opened in 1771, it consists of seven main arches, which carry the road high above the river, and an additional 'dry' arch on either side to cope with floods. It is built of old red sandstone from Quarrymill, about half a mile up river, and contains 'oculi' filled with black stone, between the arches. In 1869 the deck was widened, and footpaths built out on metal brackets, which also support the elegant cast iron lamp standards. Standing over the keystone of the main arch, high above the water,

affords a very fine view of the river, of Stanners Island, and the two more modern bridges downstream.

The peak river levels reached during each of the major floods since 1814 are recorded on the 'dry' arch where the bridge reaches the North Inch.

## Earlier Bridges

Smeaton's bridge was not, of course, the first bridge over the Tay at Perth. In mediaeval times there was a timber bridge, continuing the line of the High Street, across Stanners Island to the east bank. The date of its construction is not known, but it was carried away in the terrible flood of 1209, which also destroyed Perth's castle, and endangered the life of the King, William 'The Lion' (see Introduction).

The bridge was replaced remarkably quickly however, because it is recorded that, in 1214, King William's funeral cortege was met on the new bridge by his son, King Alexander II. Although we know very little about this second bridge,

Flood levels carved on the 'dry' arch.

apart from accounts for its repairs, it stood the test of time, lasting nearly 400 years, before collapsing in 1607. This is the bridge shown in David Simon's picture (see Chapter 2).

In 1604, with the bridge in poor condition, King James VI engaged John Mylne to build a replacement a few yards upstream, and this was completed in 1616. However, the

### Perth Bridge Toll House

In 1870 a tollhouse was erected on the eastern approach to the bridge. Fixed to the tollhouse is the proclamation of a local Bye Law, dated 1879, the relevant part of which states 'that no locomotive shall pass on or over the Perth Bridge between the hours of 10 am and 3 pm… at other times the person in charge of such locomotive shall send a man with a red flag to the opposite end of the bridge warning all persons concerned of the approach of the locomotive'. 'Health and Safety' was alive and well 150 years ago.

Notice on the Toll House of Perth Bridge.

At low tide, during times of drought, the line of the 1616 bridge can still be made out by turbulence in the water over the stumps of the old piers.

Ford over the river. Paved track leading from the Lynedoch Memorial on the river bank into the water.
MAP 1 · P13

**A Roman Bridge:** Depictions on Roman coins dating from the invasion of Caledonia in 208-209 AD, by the Emperor Septimus Severus, raise the tantalising prospect of a timber bridge across the Tay from the huge Roman fort at Carpow, some five miles down stream from Perth, to the opposite bank near the present village of St Madoes.

replacement grew, and eventually the Earl of Kinnoull, the Government and the people of Perth itself provided the funds, and John Smeaton was engaged to build it.

On a fine summer afternoon, looking at the bridge, it is difficult to imagine that all the space underneath the high arches could possibly be required for water. And yet in February 1774, during Scotland's 'Little Ice Age', just three years after it was completed, a thaw following a prolonged cold spell brought huge ice flows down the river. They became wedged beneath the arches, creating a dam and causing the flooding of large areas of the town. The bridge, however, remained intact.

arches were low, and only five years later, in 1621, the bridge was carried away in another dreadful flood.

For the next 150 years, Perth had no bridge. When the water is low, it was, and still is, possible to ford the river from the North Inch on horseback. However, the general dependence on ferries seriously hampered the town's development. Gradually pressure to build a

## Railway Bridge

The 19th century brought two more bridges to Perth. The first wooden railway bridge was built in 1849, but was replaced by the present bridge in 1862. It carries the line to Dundee on a long curve, with ten arches in the central section arising from Moncrieffe Island, and 11 wrought iron spans over the water. The span nearest to Tay Street is wider than the

Train emerging from the treetops on the Island section of the bridge, and approaching the east bank of the river. St Matthew's spire in the background.
MAP 1 · T2

rest, and used to accommodate a swing bridge, to allow tall-masted ships to access the harbour. When the line reaches the Perth bank, it crosses above Tay Street and then on a viaduct behind the elegant Georgian houses of Marshall Place to the railway station.

## Queen's Bridge

In 1898 Perth acquired its second road bridge, continuing the line of South Street across the river. Called the Victoria Bridge, it was replaced in 1960 by the Queen's Bridge, a light, triple-span, pre-stressed concrete construction. This bridge was opened by HM the Queen on the 750th anniversary of the Royal Charter granted to Perth by King William the Lion.

## Friarton Bridge

The last of Perth's bridges, the Friarton Bridge, carries the M90 from Edinburgh to Dundee and Aberdeen high above the Tay about a mile south of Perth city centre. Completed in 1978, it was the first lightweight concrete bridge built in Europe.

### Railway Footpath

The railway bridge also carries a footpath, which provides the only regular access to Moncrieffe Island, with its allotments and unique King James VI Golf Course. This footpath facilitates a pleasant circular walk, from Tay Street, over the railway bridge, through the parks on the east bank of the river and back over the Perth Bridge to Tay Street.

# CHAPTER FOUR

# Perth's Flood Defences

## Why the River Tay Floods

Two factors cause flooding of the Tay at Perth. The first is the amount of water flowing off the hills into the river. The Tay is by far the largest river in the United Kingdom, discharging more water into the sea than the Thames and Severn combined.

The Tay catchment is divided into five distinct areas, drained by the five main rivers in the system – the Almond, the Tay itself, the Tummel, the Garry and the Isla. The effects of the weather fronts as they pass across Scotland are felt in the various areas at different times. The resulting peak flows in each river will last for only a short time, and will take several hours to pass down river. Perth is at risk when the peak flows from all of them arrive at the same time. That is what happened in 1993.

The second factor is the tide. The Tay estuary stretches for some 35 miles from its mouth between Buddon Ness and Tentsmuir to Perth, and the river is still tidal as far as its junction with the Almond. When deep low pressure systems pass over the North Sea, they raise the sea level, and may also produce strong winds from the east or north-east, which pile up the water in the long estuarial funnel. When these factors occur at a time of high spring tides, the coastal strip of the Tay estuary and Perth itself are at risk of flooding.

Fortunately, in modern times, the river factors and tidal factors have not coincided.

## The 1993 Flood

Flood levels in Perth are regularly compared to that of the 1814 flood, which reached seven metres 'Above Ordnance Datum' (AOD), as marked on the dry arch of Smeaton's Bridge (see picture in Chapter 3). In 1990 there was the most severe flood since 1814, with the level at Smeaton's Bridge reaching 5.85 metres AOD. There was widespread flooding in the Tay Valley, but the defences around Perth, constructed in 1974, were just adequate. This, and the slightly less severe flood of 1989, prompted the first moves to strengthen Perth's defences and institute a system of flood warnings.

The flood on 17 January 1993 came before any flood protection measures were constructed, but the flood warning system was generally effective, and prevented the loss of livestock, and reduced the damage to property. The river level on that day reached 6.48 metres AOD, still half a metre short of the 1814 level. At the Ballathie gauging station, eight miles north of Perth, the highest ever flow

### Flood clusters

Tay floods tend to come in clusters. In the last century there have been three notable clusters, with flood levels above 5.0 metres AOD. They were in 1909, 1910, 1912, and 1913; in 1947, 1950 and 1951; and the most recent cluster in 1989, 1990 and 1993. This clustering is unexplained.

on a UK river was recorded, (2,268 m3s-1). The centre of Perth and the Inches were flooded, with water coming over the western end of the Queen's Bridge. Around the Museum and Art Gallery the water was several feet deep, and parts of the North Muirton housing estate were inundated to a depth of six feet. Over 1,500 homes in the city were flooded, 1,200 of them in Muirton. Millions of pounds worth of damage was caused.

There were two factors, however, which ameliorated the severity of the flooding in 1990 and 1993. The first was the management of the water levels behind the dams of the Tummel-Garry and the Breadalbane hydroelectric schemes, and the second, more important, was that both floods coincided with low tides. It might have been worse.

The centre of Perth a few hours after the peak of the 1993 flood.
© Perth & Kinross Council.

Peak of the 1993 flood. Site of the new Concert Hall.
© Perth & Kinross Council.

# Perth's Flood Defence Scheme

On 29 October 2001, the new flood defence scheme was opened. It was the result of four years of hydrological studies, research and design work, followed by four years of building. It was the largest project of its type in Scotland, and had cost £25m. It consists of eight kilometres of floodwalls and embankments, stretching from the confluence of the Rivers Almond and Tay in the north, to the harbour at Friarton in the south, together with pumps and flood storage areas on the South Inch and

at Broxden to contain flows from tributaries. There are 80 floodgates, some over six feet high, and removable flood barriers at the promontory and at the Queen's Bridge. It is designed to provide protection from flooding levels equivalent to the 1814 flood plus 300–400 mm of 'freeboard' to protect against wave action.

## View the Flood Defences

The various barriers and gates can best be seen by walking along Tay Street from the North Inch to the Railway Bridge. One of the objectives of the scheme was to enhance the appearance of Perth's already attractive riverfront. To this end, adjusting the camber of the road, and so raising the riverside pavement by nearly two feet, reduced the height of the necessary floodwall to about four feet, enabling pedestrians to look over the wall and see the river.

The floodwall is of dressed sandstone, polished on the street side, and supported by 35 square pillars topped with pyramidal caps in late Georgian style. Fifteen of these were decorated with sculpted panels by artist, Gillian Forbes when the wall was built in 2001. Many of the carvings feature icons representing Perth's history, its fauna, flora, people and places; others pinpoint historical sites, and several are incised with texts from William Soutar's poems.

In 2011 and 2012, a further five pillars were decorated, also by Gillian Forbes, with the coats of arms of Perth's twin towns – Aschaffenburg in Germany, Cognac in France, Bydgoszcz in Poland, Pskov in Russia and Perth in Canada.

Most of the pillars are referred to elsewhere in the text, but it is appropriate to include a list below, beginning at the flood gates near the 'dry' arch. Where the pillars are illustrated elsewhere, the chapter is referenced. Others are pictured below.

**Unthank** 'Unthank' was a farm within the boundary of mediaeval Perth. Potatoes are the crop. Unthank was a common farm name in the early 20th century.

**Douglas** Plant hunter, David Douglas (see Chapter 12).

GATE IN THE WALL

**Mousetrap** Mousetrap pool. *John MacNab*, novel by John Buchan.

**Tayberry** The tayberry, a cross between a raspberry and a bramble (blackberry) was bred by the Scottish Horticultural Research Institute in Invergowrie, East Perthshire.

**Blue Kinnoull** A variety of *Meconopsis* (the blue poppy).

**Aschaffenburg** Coat of arms of Perth's twin city in Bavaria (see Chapter 1).

**Cognac** Coat of arms of Perth's twin city in France. (see Chapter 1)

PROMONTORY

**Site of the mediaeval Perth Bridge.**

**Pskov** Coat of arms of Perth's twin city in western Russia (see Chapter 1).

BLANK PILLAR

**Bydgoszcz** Coat of Arms of Perth's twin city in Poland (see Chapter 1).

**Site of the Glovers' dance platform** (see Chapter 19).

**Perth Canada** Coat of Arms of Perth's twin town in Canada (see Chapter 8).

**The Earth** Part of a poem, 'Autobiography' by William Soutar (see Chapter 7).

**Pearl mussel** Fresh water pearl mussels used to be fished from the Tay (see Chapter 8).

**Gibralter** Quay on the east bank of the river (see Chapter 13).

**Heart of Scotland** 'Heart of Scotland' (see Chapter 1).

GATE IN THE WALL

**Cream of the Well** Relates to the five springs at Pitkeathly Wells, west of Bridge of Earn. The springs were said to cure everything from psoriasis to kidney stones, and

'Unthank' was a farm within the boundary of the mediaeval burgh of Perth.

The tayberry. The soft fruit industry is very important in east Perthshire.

The text incised into the stone reads, 'The Old Perth Bridge spanned the river near this point. It was destroyed by a flood in 1621'.

Cream of the Well. Relates to the village of Pitkeathly Wells.

were especially effective if the patient had walked to Pitkeathly Wells from Perth before breakfast! (about five miles).

QUEEN'S BRIDGE

TEN BLANK PILLARS

GATE IN THE WALL

BLANK PILLAR

**Monk's Tower** Opposite Canal Street, is the site of Monk's Tower (see Chapter 2).

**'Aince Upon a Day'** Verse 1 of the poem by William Soutar (see Chapter 7).

**'Aince Upon a Day'** Verse 2 of the poem by William Soutar. (see Chapter 7).

FOUR BLANK PILLARS

SLIPWAY to the river.

The pavement itself is broad and consists of high quality flagstones, punctuated by flowerbeds, trees and benches.

As well as the Pillar Sculptures, Tay Street is enlivened by several other small works of art. Opposite Canal Street, a railing along the top of the floodwall is decorated with Ronda Bailey's quirky bronzes of animal forms, *Soutar's Menagerie*,

*Top right:*

Ronda Bailey's *Soutar's Menagerie*, inspired by illustrations from Soutar's bairn-rhymes.

*Left:*

Lee Brewster's *The Salmon Run*.

*Right:*

David Annand's *Goldeneye on the Dark and Singing Tide*.

from his bairn-rhymes. Opposite the Sheriff Court is *The Salmon Run* by Lee Brewster (2003), a bench with a wavy aluminium back, pierced by images of leaping salmon. Farther up the street, on the corner of Tay Street and the Queen's Bridge is a bronze by David Annand (2002), *Goldeneye on the Dark and Singing Tide*. It is a complicated but interesting work, featuring a duck half submerged, foraging among the stones of the

riverbed. Finally, near to the Perth Bridge, is the bronze *Eagle of Perth* by Shona Kinloch (2003).

There are three gaps in the floodwall to allow fishermen and others to access steps leading down to the river. Unless the river level is high, the heavy floodgates are open, and the gap in the wall is filled with mild steel gates featuring motifs representing the surrounding landscape and wildlife, designed by Malcolm Robertson.

In the corner of the South Inch car park opposite the Fergusson Gallery is an abstract sculpture in metal on a stone plinth – *Fish with a Boy* by Doug Cocker (1995).

## Perth's Memorial Garden

Leave Tay Street by the two low floodgates, leading down to the 'dry' arch and the North Inch, then pass the large double gate which protects

the rear of the houses and offices in Charlotte Street to reach Perth's memorial garden and outdoor war memorials. These lie in a hollow created by the floodwall and embankment and are not protected from flooding. The memorials are described in Chapter 18.

Clockwise:

*The Eagle of Perth*, bronze by Shona Kinloch.

The gap in the wall is closed at times of flood risk by heavy flood gates.

*Fish with a Boy*, in the South Inch car park.
MAP 1 · P2

Decorative gates close the gap in the floodwall.

## The North Inch

From the Memorial Garden, pass through the two huge floodgates which protect the North Inch. They have massive bronze decorations: *River Tay Themes* by David Wilson. On the 'dry' (city) side of these floodgates are another two bronze panels in the floodwall. One shows the Lynedoch obelisk, surrounded by floodwater, with the Perth Bridge in the background. The other shows a representation of Perth Castle (see Chapter 2), which stood near this

*Clockwise:*

The floodgates leading to the Dry Arch and the North Inch.

One of the bronze gates at the Memorial Garden. *River Tay Themes*, by David Wilson.
MAP 1 · P12

Bronze plaque on the floodwall at the North Inch showing Lynedoch Obelisk and the Perth Bridge during a flood.
MAP 1 · P12

Victorian mansion on the east bank of the river, looking across to the North Inch.

Once a year, early on a Sunday morning in September, all the gates and barriers are inspected, and then closed in a test to make sure everything is in working order.

spot, but was swept away in the floods of 1209.

From these gates, a broad embankment, running nearly five kilometres to the mouth of the River Almond protects the North Inch, the adjacent houses and businesses, and the North Muirton housing estate, which suffered so severely in 1993. Along the crest of the embankment there is a foot and cycle path which affords good views of the river and the Georgian and early Victorian villas on the opposite bank.

## The Red Brig and the Lade

Those interested in the difficulties encountered controlling the water level in the Lade, which runs through the protected area of the city and discharges directly into the Tay,

should visit the Red Brig, opposite the Concert Hall. There the Lade is contained by three gates, the largest of which has an elaborate bronze decoration. Look down into the Lade's deep channel and speculate on the situation should its water level approach the lip of the gates.

## Awards

Perth's flood defence scheme is the largest and most comprehensive in Scotland. It was immediately hailed as an engineering and aesthetic triumph and has won many awards. Delegations of engineers, architects and planners still visit it. So far, however, it has not been tested.

The Red Brig opposite the Concert Hall, where the Lade can be seen in a deep channel. MAP 1 · O11

One of three floodgates at the Red Brig. These contain the backflow of the river into the Lade.

# Whisky and Perth

By the end of the 18th century, distilling had become a recognisable industry in Scotland, but with two distinct elements. In the arable Lowlands, distilling was pursued on a relatively large scale, using the patented Coffey Still, and much of the product was sold to England. Robert Burns referred to this product as 'a most rascally liquor'. By contrast, in the Highlands the industry was fragmented, with many pot stills producing small volumes of malt whiskies with much stronger tastes, but of variable quality.

In the 19th and early 20th centuries, three entrepreneurial local families were able to exploit Perth's geographical position between the Highlands and the Lowlands and establish whisky dynasties, which together identified Perth as the

whisky capital of Scotland. All three started out as licensed grocers or wine merchants – Matthew Gloag in 1800; Arthur Bell in 1825; and John Dewar in 1843. These three, along with others from similar backgrounds elsewhere in Scotland, began the development of Scotch whisky from what might now be called a farm diversification enterprise into the global industry it now is.

The innovation that they pioneered was blending. They were not distillers. They bought in the whiskies, mixing the lighter, cheaper grain whisky with the stronger flavoured malts to produce a drink

Matthew Gloag's original shop in Atholl Street, Perth.
© The Edrington Group.

The whisky companies traded on the reputation of the Scottish regiments.
© John Dewar & Sons Ltd.

DEWAR'S "White Label" SCOTCH WHISKY never varies

'Celebrate with the finest drink in the world'

that was affordable, palatable, and importantly, consistent. This appealed in particular to the burgeoning market in the south. To their skills with the *water of life* all three families added marketing genius, which was able to capitalise on the development of the British Empire, the importance of the Highland regiments in the British Army, and the enthusiasm, inspired by Sir Walter Scott and embraced by Queen Victoria, for all things Scottish. They were also fortunate that the French brandy industry collapsed in the second half of the 19th century, due to infestation with *phylloxera*, an insect similar to an aphid, which devastated the vineyards and left a huge gap in the market.

## The Dewar Whisky Barons

Of the three families, John Dewar's two sons, John Alexander (later Lord Forteviot) and Thomas (later Lord Dewar of Homestall) were the most spectacularly successful, but left the smallest footprint in Perth. John Alexander stayed in Perth to manage the production of the whisky, while Thomas (Tommy) went to London to develop the brand. Tommy was a born publicist, and coined many of advertising's most well known slogans. Among them are, 'If you don't advertise, you fossilise', and 'You keep advertising, and advertising will keep you'.

However, in 1925 Dewar's was absorbed into the Distillers Company Ltd and were later taken over by Guinness. In 1988 the enormous bonded warehouse and offices near the railway

Dewar's was the most spectacularly successful of the Perth whisky firms.
© John Dewar & Sons Ltd.

Dewar's enormous bonded warehouse and offices adjacent to the railway station.
© John Dewar & Sons Ltd.

station were closed and demolished, the site taken by the Perth Leisure Pool, and the Dewar's Centre (see Chapter 15), and this was followed in 1994 by the closure of the Inveralmond bottling plant. When Guinness and Grand Metropolitan came together to form Diageo in 1997, the Competitions Authority insisted on the disposal of the Dewar's brand, which was purchased by the Bacardi Group in the largest brand sale ever.

Apart from the Forteviot Charitable Trust, which disburses around £200,000 per year, much of it to Perthshire charities, and Kinnoull Hill, given to the City by Lord (Tommy) Dewar, there is now little evidence of any legacy from the Dewar's whisky business.

## Matthew Gloag and 'The Famous Grouse'

The Gloags were the only Perth whisky family not to brand their products with the family name. In 1896, Matthew, the third generation of the Gloag family, decided to market a new blend by appealing directly to the 'hunting, shooting, fishing' fraternity of Victorian Britain, naming it 'The Grouse'. His daughter, Phillipa, drew the famous Red Grouse that still features on the label. It was an immediate success, and in 1905, to reinforce that popularity, he relaunched it on the 'Glorious 12th of August' as 'The Famous Grouse'. The brand has never looked back and since 1980 it has been Scotland's best selling whisky.

Two World Wars, prohibition in the United States and the recession in the 1930s, failed to impede Matthew Gloag's progress. However, by 1970, crippling death duties and the necessity to rationalise the industry forced Matthew Gloag to sell to Highland Distillers, which owned several of the distilleries that produced the malt whiskies in the Famous Grouse blend. In 1999 in a further bout of rationalisation, Edrington Distillers of Glasgow, an independent company owned by the Robertson Trust, bought the company.

In 1996 Highland Distillers built a splendid new headquarters for their business on a greenfield site at Kinfauns, on the eastern outskirts of Perth overlooking the Tay. This building now houses a major part of the marketing division of Edrington,

**The Robertson Trust** is a charitable organisation established in 1961 by the three Robertson sisters, descendents of the founder of the company, to ensure the long term independence of their interests, which were mainly in whisky, and to continue their tradition of charitable giving. It is now the largest independent grant-giving trust in Scotland, and in 2012 distributed £15.3m to charity.

and employs around 100 people. While there are several distilleries in Perthshire, the Kinfauns building is the only toehold that the City of Perth now has in the industry that was once so important to its economy and to its psyche.

Famous Grouse are regular supporters of events in Perth, such as the Highland Games and the Perth Show, and their mascot, Gilbert, takes part in many of the parades. The company's contribution to the celebrations of the 800th anniversary of the King William the Lion Charter, which confirmed Perth's Royal Burgh status in 2010, was a spectacular statue of a grouse taking flight, situated in the centre of the Broxden roundabout, one of the main routes into Perth (see Chapter 15).

## Bell's Whisky and the Gannochy Trust

The whisky company that has left the most substantial legacy to Perth is undoubtedly Bell's. Established as a wine merchant in 1825, by the 1840s

the company developed into a modest whisky business under the ownership of Robert Fitzroy Bell and his son Arthur. It flourished under the third generation, Arthur Kinmond Bell and Robert Bell, who built Bell's into a worldwide brand. Following the First World War, Robert withdrew from the business, but 'AK' developed it steadily despite prohibition and the depression until he died in 1942. After the Second World War the company grew phenomenally, especially between 1974 and 1984,

under the flamboyant Raymond Miquel, before succumbing to a hostile takeover bid by Guinness in 1985, later to become Diageo.

Despite promises to maintain the company headquarters in Perth, the business in Perth was steadily dismantled and by the late 1990s there was nothing left. Moreover, Bell's Whisky has not been a priority at Diageo, resulting in the current sales worldwide languishing at about half of what they were in 1985. Nevertheless, it is still said to be the most popular brand in the UK, though not in Scotland, where Famous Grouse reigns supreme.

## The Gannochy Estate

In 1922 AK Bell purchased the farm and lands of Gannochy just to the north of Bridgend with the purpose of building a housing estate (see map, Chapter 13). He had strong views about healthy living and the benefits of exercise, diet and fresh air, and so his purpose was to build a model housing scheme for his working people. Over the next ten years, 150 detached cottages, mostly three-bedroomed, were built in red sandstone. Although all were similar, each was subtly different, and set in a large garden (to permit the growing of vegetables), bounded by well-trimmed beech hedges. Neville Chamberlain, the Chancellor of the Exchequer at the time, visited the Gannochy Estate and found it to be 'unique in character, and certainly the best I have ever seen'. This was Perth's 'sunshine suburb', with most of the cottages facing south-west to

Gannochy village green and cottages.
MAP 2 · H4

Gannochy cottage with duck pond and a swan's nest.

catch the evening sun when the men returned from work. The estate is still administered by the Gannochy Trust (see below) and maintained to a very high standard, and the houses are in great demand.

## Cricket in Perth

Cricket was probably introduced into Scotland by English soldiers garrisoned here in the early 19th century. The game was recorded in Kelso in the Borders in 1820, and in Perth soon after. AK Bell was a keen sportsman, and his particular love was cricket, at which he excelled. In 1924 he bought Kincarrathie House and grounds, on the west side of the Scone Road. He used the house as his main residence, and developed the northern part of the grounds as Doo'cot Park, with a pavilion and two cricket pitches – said to be among the best in Scotland (see map, Chapter 13).

The pavilion was built in 1925 in an Edwardian Arts and Crafts style. It has a larch clad upper floor, and pantiled ogee roof, giving it an English county appearance, probably befitting a cricket club. The doo-cot, now restored, is dated 1694 and carries the initials WSB and ISR. Nearby is the 19th century garden folly or wash-house, known as the chapel.

## The Gannochy Trust

AK was childless, but he counted the citizens of Perth as his family, and left them a legacy, from which they and indeed the people of Scotland are still benefitting. This was the Gannochy Trust, the funds from which were to be used 'for certain charitable and public purposes for the benefit of the people of Perth and District'. In 1967 a scheme of alteration expanded the footprint of the donations to the whole of Scotland, but with a preference for Perth and District. In 2012 the total value of the grants disbursed was £3.9m. Included in the legacy were the Gannochy Housing Estate, Bellwood and Quarrymill parks.

Doo'cot Park Cricket pavilion. Kincarrathie House behind. MAP 2 · H4

The doo'cot in Doo'cot Park.

# After Whisky

Employment in the whisky industry in Perth declined steadily during the 1980s and 1990s as, one by one, the big companies transferred first ownership and then many hundreds of jobs out of Perth. This might have had a catastrophic effect on Perth's economy, but the city has weathered the storms very well, with unemployment consistently around a half to two-thirds of the Scottish average. This has not been achieved by securing any major inward investments from overseas or elsewhere in the UK. There are a small number of very large businesses, including Scottish and Southern Electricity, Aviva, Highland Spring and Stagecoach, but in general Perth's economy is based on small to medium sized enterprises. Many select Perth as a base because of its central position in Scotland. An example is the Royal National Lifeboat Institution. Perthshire has no coast, and certainly no lifeboats, but the RNLI has stationed its Scottish headquarters in Perth because of its hub position in the transport network.

Kincarrathie House is administered by a new trust as a retirement home.

There is hardly an aspect of life in Perth and Kinross that is untouched by the Gannochy Trust. It gives capital and revenue grants to sport, culture and the arts, music of all types, literature, horticulture, and even contributed a third of the cost of the city's new sewage works. A list of the major capital works in Perth supported by the Trust includes Bell's Sports centre, the AK Bell Library, Perth Concert Hall, Balhousie Castle, St John's Kirk and Perth Theatre. And yet, almost as important are the small revenue grants to pipe bands, sports clubs, choirs and orchestras, bloom committees, festivals of one sort or another – the list is endless. There is no doubt that the quality of life of all the citizens of Perth and Kinross, and many others across Scotland, has been significantly improved by the Gannochy Trust.

# CHAPTER SIX

# Perth's Earliest Streets

In mediaeval times Perth's main streets consisted of the High Street and South Street, stretching from the river to the city wall in the west, and two other streets, the Skinnergate and the Watergate, connecting the centre of the city with the gates (or ports) in the wall to the north and south respectively. In addition there was a maze of narrow, crowded vennels, lanes, closes and pends (see 'Overview of the City' in the Introduction). The commercial heart consisted of the harbour and the adjacent quays, and the bridge across the Tay; all clustered around the foot of the High Street (see David Simon's map, Chapter 2). Downstream there were gardens belonging to the houses along the Watergate, some with beaches and jetties, and then a smaller harbour at the canal basin where Canal Street now is. With roads almost nonexistent, the huge bulk of commercial traffic entered and left Perth by the harbour. What traffic did come to Perth by road entered the town at one of the ports in the city wall, and then negotiated the narrow, congested streets to reach the markets clustered in the centre.

The streets nearest the river were the Watergate and Skinnergate, giving access to the heart of the Burgh from south and north respectively. These streets, along with the eastern parts of the High Street

and South Street, and the closes and vennels connecting them to each other, the riverfront and the precinct of the High Kirk are the oldest parts of Perth.

Most of the mediaeval buildings have been destroyed, some quite recently and inexcusably, but a little remains, though mostly in poor condition. Elsewhere on these streets there has been a succession of new construction resulting in many elegant Georgian and Victorian buildings.

## Watergate

From the port in the city wall adjacent to Greyfriars Harbour (see David Simon's painting, Chapter 2), Speygate and Watergate carried traffic to the centre of Perth, with its markets and bridge over the river. Watergate is connected to the precinct of St John's Kirk by Baxters and Oliphants Vennels, and to the River (now Tay Street) by Water Vennel and North Boat Vennel,

Street sign.

View of the steeple of St John's Kirk from Baxters Vennel.

Gowrie House. Top panel of
the bronze plaque on the
Sheriff Court.

which together formed the heart of
the earliest Perth community. In
mediaeval times, important mansions
occupied the east side of the street,
with long narrow gardens sloping
down to the riverfront. These
included Gowrie House and the Earl
of Kinnoull's Lodging House, both
built in the early 1520s. The Lodging
House survived until 1966, but
Gowrie House was demolished in
1807 to make way for the new
Sheriff Court. Confusingly, a terrace
of buildings in Tay Street, not strictly
on the same site as the original
Gowrie House, has been given its
name (see Chapter 9).

Some old buildings, though much
modernised, still exist at the High
Street end of the Watergate, including
Nos 21 to 27. No. 25 features a
Roman Doric doorway with the date
1725. No. 23, its neighbour, dates

No. 25 of Nos 21-27
Watergate. A Roman Doric
pilastered and broken
pedimented doorpiece, now
in poor condition.
MAP 1 · P9

## The Gowrie Conspiracy

Gowrie House was the location of one
of Scotland's great mysteries. The least
improbable and best validated of
several conflicting accounts of the
events that happened on 5 August
1600 is that given by the King,
James VI. In his statement, which was
read in churches throughout Scotland,
he claimed that he was riding near
Falkland in the morning, when the
younger brother of John Ruthven, the
third Earl of Gowrie, met him and told
him of a stranger who had been
discovered in Perth with a pot of
gold coins.

The King rode immediately to Perth,
arriving at Gowrie House at about
1.00 pm. After dining amicably with the
Earl and his brother, the King was
shown into a turret room, where,
instead of meeting the man with the
gold, he was brutally attacked.
However, he managed to get to a
window and shout, 'Treason, Murder!'
to his retinue below. In the ensuing
scuffle both the Ruthven brothers
were killed.

Following the Gowrie conspiracy the
Earl of Gowrie's properties were
confiscated by the Crown. Sir George
Hay, who was present in Gowrie House
at the time, received lands at
Nethercliffe, and later became the first
Earl of Kinnoull. Sir David Murray,
cup-bearer to the King, received the
lands and mediaeval house at Scone
(later to become Scone Palace). His
descendant, the Earl of Mansfield, lives
there still (see Chapter 12).

*The Earl of Kinnoull's Lodging House in the Watergate*, by Joseph Milne.
© Perth Museum & Art Gallery, Perth & Kinross Council.

*Top:*
Fountain Close. Insignia of the
Incorporation of Tailors.
MAP 1 · P7

Celtic Cross at the end of
Fountain Close, where it used
to lead to the town house of
the Bishops of Dunkeld.

*Opposite page, top right:*
The late 18th century shop
window of AS Deuchar.

7 SCOTS, 'The Black Watch TA'
battalion marching past the
Salutation hotel after
receiving Freedom of Perth in
2010.
MAP 1 · P7
© Angus Findlay Photography.

from a century later and is much
more elaborate. The Wrights'
Incorporation used to meet in this
building.

## Fountain Close

Running parallel to the Watergate
and opening off the north side of
South Street is the blind alley of
Fountain Close. This ancient route
between South Street and Baxters
Vennel led at one time to the 15th
century townhouse of the Bishops of
Dunkeld, in the garden of which was
a fountain. Nowadays, sadly, it is no
more than a dead-end between two
shop fronts. However, its walls are
plastered and contain a number of
interesting stencils, including
representations of the crests of
Perth's various guilds, a depiction of
Gowrie House, and a Celtic cross.
These were created in 1975 by
primary school pupils from Kinnoull
School, led by their teacher Miss
Rhoda Fothergill (recently awarded
the British Empire Medal for her
services to Perth) and the art teacher
Mr WA Robson.

## South Street

Opposite Fountain Close on South
Street is the bow-fronted shop
window of the antiques dealer, AS
Deuchar. This window dates from
about 1780, and is a very rare
example of its type, possibly the last
surviving original one in Scotland. It
marks a stage in the development of
shop fronts, when glass began to be
used to close in and shelter what had
previously been an open area.

Barlass Ironmonger's shop had a similar double bow window shop front at No 58 High Street. When the building was demolished in 1963, the front was rescued and is now in the Perth Museum.

Because of the small size of glass panes available, such windows featured multiple panes of rippling crown glass. This business has been in the hands of the Deuchar family since 1911.

The Salutation Hotel faces the southern end of St John Street, and makes a fine full stop to that street. It claims to be the oldest established hotel in Scotland, and that is supported by the date 1699 on a fireplace in what is now called the

Stuart Room, which was used by Bonny Prince Charlie as his campaign HQ during his march south to the battle of Prestonpans. Moreover, for many years, a stone bearing the date 1619 and the arms of David Murray, a wealthy businessman in Perth, used to be in the courtyard. It is now in the Perth Museum and Art Gallery.

However, the hotel's glorious façade, with its magnificent Venetian window (which lights a splendid vaulted restaurant), is more recent and dates from 1800. At the time of writing, the exterior of the hotel and the painted statues of a Black Watch drum major and an officer of the Regiment certainly need to be spruced up. Nevertheless. It still lives up to John Gifford's description of it (in the *Perth and Kinross* volume of 'The Buildings of Scotland') as 'Perth's swankiest late Georgian building'.[1]

## The Route from Castle to Kirk – the Skinnergate and Kirkgate

The Castle, built on a mound near to the present Museum and Art Gallery, would have been home for a large number of people, especially when the King was in residence. And so in the 11th and 12th centuries, the processional route from the Castle to the High Kirk for Mass, and other religious ceremonies, was well trodden. It led from the Castle, over

Stuart Room fireplace, dated 1699, in the Salutation Hotel.

Statue of a Black Watch drum major on the Salutation Hotel façade.

Statue of a Black Watch Officer on the Salutation Hotel façade.

1  *Perth and Kinross* by John Gifford. 'The Buildings of Scotland', Yale University Press, p. 635.

the Lade and through the Red Brig Port in the city wall, to the Skinnergate, and then across the High Street and via Kirkgate, to St John's Kirk. The Red Brig Port was also the route into the city for all traffic from the north.

While the Watergate was where the wealthy and titled lived and the Wrights' Incorporation was based, the Skinnergate, as it name implies, was associated with the tanning industry, and was an altogether less salubrious environment. It was however, the base for the Glovers' Incorporation, which was one of the largest and most influential guilds in Perth.

Nothing of the mediaeval Skinnergate remains, but there is one building on the east side which harks back to its ancient origins – the Old Ship Inn. This pub, said to date from 1665, used to have access to the foreshore and quays adjacent to the harbour, and was indeed a dockside pub for a hundred years, until George Street was built and cut it off

from the river. The present building, however, is late Victorian, in red sandstone with crow-stepped gables.

Adjacent to the Old Ship Inn are several posters, erected by the Scottish Urban Archaeological Trust, purporting to report on major events in Perth's history, as they might have been told by an imaginary local newspaper, the *Perthshire Advertiser*.

Two other buildings in Skinnergate are worth looking at. On the west side is Skinnergate House, a well-proportioned neo-Georgian, red-brick building dating from 1927. It was built as a model lodging house, and is now the Salvation Army's resettlement unit. It has been refurbished recently, and is in very good condition. Also, at the north end of the street, overlooking the Red Brig and the Concert Hall, is the controversial 21st century glass and steel extension into the Skinnergate of Gillies's furniture shop.

The Kirkgate was one of the 'Kirk Vennels'. It connected the precinct of the Kirk to the High Street, at the point where the Mercat Cross was situated. It was once an important thoroughfare, being on the main route from the Castle to the Kirk. Royalty would regularly process

Skinnergate House.
Salvation Army lodging house.
MAP 1 · O10

The steel and glass extension to Gillies's furniture store. Rotary Clock is in the foreground.
MAP 1 · O11

Marriage lintel above the entrance to King's Arms Close, 15 High Street.
MAP 1 · Q10

along this route to say Mass, or attend religious festivals.

## King's Arms or Cunningham-Graham Close

Contemporaneous with the now demolished mediaeval buildings of the Skinnergate is the building above Kings Arms Close. This is the oldest inhabited building in Perth. The close leads between two much altered shops at No 15 High Street to the rear of the tenement where at one time there was the King's Arms Inn. Above the pend is a sculpted and painted pediment with the marriage initials RG EC, and the date 1699.

On the keystone of the pend is the heraldic emblem of a rather grim head with a coronet, and at the sides, painted scallop shells. The initials stand for Robert Graham (at one time the Town Clerk of Perth) and Elspeth Cunningham. The coronet alludes to Graham's relative, James, First Marquis of Montrose.

The property was in a very poor condition, but an Historic Building Grant was secured through the Perth City Heritage Fund, to enable the close and stairwell to be restored and the flats above made habitable once again, so breathing life back into this ancient part of Perth.

## Meal Vennel

(See David Simon's painting, Chapter 2.) Before King Edward Street was built, Meal Vennel was an ancient and important thoroughfare connecting the High Street and South Street. All traces of it were erased when the St John's Centre was built. The through route was preserved by entrances to the Centre from both streets, as well as connections to Kinnoull Street and King Edward Street, so that pedestrians could walk the route of the vennel. However, it was closed recently when the shops on South Street were refurbished.

This house, above the Kings Arms Close, later became the town house of Viscount Stormont of Scone. It was here that Prince Charles Edward Stuart lodged in 1745 during his eight-day sojourn in Perth. Meanwhile the King's Arms Inn became the base for the Jacobite army.

CHAPTER SEVEN

# The Commercial Heart of Perth

## High Street and South Street

High Street and South Street were the two major thoroughfares of mediaeval Perth, each running from the river in the east to gates in the city wall in the west. Connecting them was the Watergate and a grid of narrow vennels which enclosed Perth's High Kirk and its precinct. Linking this central core to the north was the Skinnergate, which ran from the High Street to the city wall at the Red Brig Port near the castle. Towards the south, Speygate continued the line of the Watergate to a port in the city wall, which opened onto Perth's second harbour at the southern outfall of the Lade (see David Simon's map, Chapter 2). While only a few traces of the mediaeval buildings remain, the basic pattern of these streets and vennels is as it was 800 years ago.

## High Street from Tay Street to George Street

### Perth's Civic Centre

The High Street was, and remains, Perth's most important street. For centuries, the harbour at the foot of the street was Perth's gateway to the world, and appropriately the Royal

Burgh's civic buildings have been situated close by since the 13th century. In mediaeval times, the Tolbooth built across the end of the High Street completely sealed off the street from the river and the harbour. Goods, whether being exported or imported, and traffic crossing the river on the bridge, had to pass through a pend in the Tolbooth, to enable duties and tolls to be collected. The Tolbooth also served as the Council Chambers, the prison, and as a meeting place for the Scottish Parliament.

The Tolbooth was demolished in 1839 and replaced in 1879 by the

Outside the Tolbooth, its position marked now by a circular stone in the road, was The Pillory, to which miscreants were tied for punishment. Here too the gallows were erected when the ultimate penalty was to be exacted.

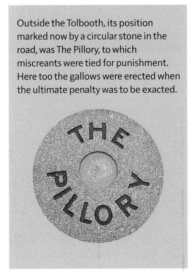

range of buildings extending from the
Middle Free Church or Red Church
on Tay Street, round the corner into
the High Street. The buildings
included the District Court, various
Council offices, and the Council
Chamber itself, facing across the
High Street. The corner of this range
features an oriel turret with slated
spire, set atop a 'fat' decorated pillar
carved with the individual quarters of
the royal arms and a thistle. This
recalls the turret on the old Tolbooth
illustrated in Alexander McLauchlan's
painting. Further up the High Street,

the line of the building is advanced
slightly to represent a tower, also
topped with an eight-sided slated
spire, which is based on a tower of
the ancient St Mary's Chapel which
stood on this site, and was for many
years Perth's 'hospital'.

## Old Council Chambers

The actual chamber where council
meetings were held, is on the first
floor. It was seriously damaged by
fire in 1895, but restored by the
original architect (A Heiton Junior).

Andrew Heiton's range of buildings extends round the corner of Tay Street and onto the High Street.

It is like a mediaeval baronial hall, with a hammer-beam roof and a huge canopied fireplace featuring a 17th century cast iron fireback, which bears the royal coat of arms. Sadly, the room is too small for modern Council meetings, which require space for Council officers, the press and the public, as well as the Councillors. And so it is now used

The eight-sided turret atop a 'fat' pillar on the corner of the old Council Chambers. MAP 1 · Q10

Interior of the old Council Chamber.

Elegant roof in the Old Council Chambers.

Roof detail. Note the insignias of the Glovers and Hammermen on the corbels.

*Top right*:
Old Council Chamber. Fire back with Royal Coat of Arrms.

*Bottom right*:
Replica portrait of John Pullar Esq, Lord Provost of Perth 1867–73. Painted by Walter Spindler 1896. Original by JM Barclar RSA.

mainly for events, especially weddings. The main interest lies in its hammer-beam roof, its portraits of past Lord Provosts, and in particular its stained-glass windows. The portraits were all destroyed in the fire, but have been replaced.

The large east window features the capture of Perth by King Robert the Bruce in 1312. On the wall facing south are depictions of the main characters in Sir Walter Scott's novel *The Fair Maid of Perth* (Chapter 16). On the stairway, the window is of a youthful Queen Victoria and Prince Albert when they visited Perth in 1842.

Outside the old Council Chambers are two blue street lamps decorated with the arms of the old City and Royal Burgh of Perth, the motto *Pro Rege, Lege, et Grege*

Stained-glass portraits of Queen Victoria and Prince Albert in 1842.

Street lights commemorating the coronation of King George VI.

Detail of commemorative street lamp.

1ST POLISH ARMY CORPS
IN GRATEFUL APPRECIATION OF
THE FRIENDSHIP EXTENDED
TO THEM IN THE
CITY AND COUNTY
OF PERTH,
WHERE THE POLISH TROOPS
AFTER UNDERGOING TRIAL
AND HARDSHIPS, WERE ABLE
TO RALLY AND CONTINUE,
WITH THEIR ALLIES, THE FIGHT
FOR FREEDOM AND LIBERTY
1940–1942

(for the King, the Law and the People), and the date 12–5–1937. They were erected to commemorate the coronation of King George VI, who was a Freeman of Perth.

## Polish Army Plaque

Beside the door of the Chambers is a bronze plaque carrying the emblem of Poland – a single-headed crowned eagle. The text reads:

PRESENTED BY
THE GENERAL COMMANDING,
OFFICERS AND MEN OF THE

After the war a large number of Polish ex-servicemen settled in Perth. A section of the Wellshill/Jeanfield cemetery was allocated for members of the Polish Armed Forces, and it now contains over 300 graves. In recent years, Perth's Polish community has received a revitalising influx of young Polish immigrants who have contributed significantly to the economy of the city and its rural hinterland.

PRESENTED BY
THE GENERAL COMMANDING
OFFICERS AND MEN OF THE
1ST POLISH ARMY CORPS
IN GRATEFUL APPRECIATION OF
THE FRIENDSHIP EXTENDED
TO THEM IN THE
CITY AND COUNTY
OF PERTH,
WHERE THE POLISH TROOPS,
AFTER UNDERGOING TRIAL
AND HARDSHIPS, WERE ABLE
TO RALLY AND CONTINUE,
WITH THEIR ALLIES, THE FIGHT
FOR FREEDOM AND LIBERTY
1940 - 1942

## New Council Chambers

Across the High Street, on the other
corner with Tay Street are the New
Council Chambers, designed by
GPK Young, and opened in 1901 as
the General Accident's prestigious
new headquarters. The building was
greatly extended in 1958, along the
High Street to the Watergate, and the
main (as opposed to the ceremonial)
entrance to the building is now on
the corner of High Street and the
Watergate. In 1983 General Accident
moved out to new premises at
Pitheavlis on the western outskirts of
Perth and the building was purchased
by the council. It is now used as the
Council's headquarters, and has the
offices of the Provost, Councillors
and senior officers. In 2015 these
offices close for an extensive
refurbishment.

### The 'GA' and Sir Francis Norie-Miller

The company that became the General
Accident Fire and Life Assurance
Corporation Limited was founded in
1885 by a group of farmers as a
consequence of the 1880 Act of
Parliament, which rendered employers
liable to compensate employees for
accidents at work. A plaque on the wall
of 44 Tay Street records that two rooms
of that building constituted the first
office of the company.

Francis Norie-Miller was the company's
first secretary. An astute risk-taker, with
a driving ambition for his company, he
developed it rapidly and internationally
and moved into the opulent new offices
a mere 16 years after the foundation of
the business. An example of Norie-
Miller's acumen was his early
appreciation of the importance of motor
insurance. He targeted motor insurance
aggressively, securing for example, the
business of the royal family by 1908. He
also arranged with the Morris Company
that every new car sold had free
insurance for a year with the GA. The
contract was a loss-leader, but he built
up valuable connections with motor
dealers right across the UK.

He was awarded the Freedom of Perth in
1933 and created Baronet of Cleeve in
1936. He stood unsuccessfully for
Parliament for the Perth constituency
1931, but captured the seat in April 1935
in a by-election, in his 76th year.
However, he held it for only a few
months, as he did not contest the
general election in the following
November. He retired as chairman of
the company in 1944, and died four
years later.

### Sir Stanley Norie-Miller

The company continued to prosper under Sir Francis's son Stanley, but eventually succumbed to the rationalisation of the insurance industry. The building at Pitheavlis is now one of several 'Centres of Excellence' in the Aviva company (see Chapter 15). Sir Stanley gifted the Norie-Miller Park on the east bank of the Tay to the people of Perth (see Chapter 13). He died in 1973 and, having no heir, the baronetcy became extinct.

The GA's large and extravagantly appointed 'Banking Hall' on the ground floor, overlooking the river, is about to be refurbished by the Council and used for official functions. A magnificent marble stair leads from the front door to the first floor. Only senior members of staff were permitted to ascend this stair to the wood-panelled Board Room, used now by the Council for small receptions, and to Sir Francis Norie-Miller's lavish General Manager's room, which is now the Provost's office.

The General Accident building flew the flag of every nation it dealt with – a colourful tradition that the Council has continued.
MAP 1 · Q9

The arched Banking Hall windows on the Tay Street frontage of the New Council Chambers.

The GA did business in over 50 countries, and the flags of many of countries were flown from the windows of the building. This custom has continued, and makes for a very colourful spectacle – enhanced during the summer by a beautiful display of floral window boxes on the ground floor.

Watergate was pedestrianised in 1990, the first such zone in Perth. In 2011 the street underwent a multi-million pound refurbishment appropriate for the most important shopping street in Perth, where all manner of shops, banks, cafés and restaurants can be found. It has a very pleasant ambience, with trees and benches, large information boards and some important public art.

Between George Street and Skinnergate on the north side, there is an impressive terrace of four storey buildings dating from the late 18th century. The first of these, on the corner, has the date 1774 high on the gable. It was restyled in 1905, at the height of the Temperance Movement, as a baker's shop and tearoom above, to enable the ladies of Perth to socialise. The elegant first floor windows with an oriel bay and Art Nouveau glass remain, although no longer used as a café.

Further up on this terrace is the shop of T Patterson, Jeweller. The current proprietor is the fifth generation of the family to have the business, which started in 1832, before Victoria came to the throne. The shop front and the clock above have been through a number of manifestations, the present one dating from 2004.

## High Street: George Street to King Edward Street

High Street. Georgian terrace between George street and Skinnergate.
MAP 1 · P9

The High Street westwards from the junction of George Street and the

Just beyond the Skinergate on the north side of the street is the VisitScotland tourist information centre.

On the south side the buildings are more mixed. The first one on the corner of the Watergate is impressive. It was built in 1788, but has been much modified and has recently had an expensive façade improvement. It faces down George Street, for which it forms an impressive full stop. It is on the site of one of the oldest houses in Perth, and was the property of the Mercers of Aldie, a prominent Perth family for 800 years. Above the central first floor window is a gilded coat of arms

showing a star, three mill wheels and three Maltese crosses, surmounted by a helmeted head and a crane with a serpent in its beak. Above it is the enigmatic inscription 'The Green House'. During the mid-18th century the 'House of Green' was an inn, presided over by one Kitty Reid. It was the unofficial headquarters of the golfing fraternity in Perth and was where they kept their clubs. The ground floor is now occupied by one of Perth's French establishments, Café Breizh. A more recent representation of the Mercer coat of arms features in a funeral hatchment in the north transept of St John's Kirk, where the Mercer family were buried.

## Mercat Cross

On the High Street, between the openings of Skinnergate and Kirkgate, stood Perth's Mercat (Market) Cross. Its position is marked in the pedestrianised street by a small stone cross. It is not known when the original Mercat

*Clockwise:*

Oriel bay window with art nouveau glass, on the corner of George Street and the High Street. The date, '1774', can be seen high on the gable.

Mixed styles of buildings on south side of the High Street.

Mercer Arms high on the restored façade above the Café Breizh.

Mercer funeral hatchment in St John's Kirk

Site of the Mercat (Market) Cross.

*Right:*
The Guildhall.
MAP 1 · H9

*Below right:*
Sculpture above middle window of Guildhall.

The shaft and surmounting lion rampant from Perth's 1669 Mercat Cross are now to be found at Fingask Castle about ten miles east of Perth, in the Carse of Gowrie. A thistle medallion, also taken from the cross, is incorporated in a marriage lintel dated 1766, with the initials LR and MB, which is sited prominently above a shop window in Fleshers Vennel between St John's Place and South Street.

Finial from Perth's Mercat Cross mounted as a marriage lintel above a shop in Fleshers Vennel.

Cross was erected, but it was a huge structure, with an internal stairway to a platform at the top. The building was demolished by Cromwell in 1651, to supply stone for his citadel.

A replacement cross was erected in 1669 and it was from this vantage point that the Young Pretender, Prince Charles Edward Stuart, proclaimed his father James Francis Edward Stuart to be King of England, Scotland and Ireland (James VIII and III) on 3 September 1745. This building was taken down in 1765, because it was impeding traffic (see Edward VII Memorial in Chapter 8).

Between the Kirkgate and the Guildhall at the opening of a close leading to the back yards of the High Street properties is a fish mosaic, which may mark the site of Perth's original fishmarket. Adjacent is a much smaller mosaic of two ears of barley.

## Guildhall

Overlooking the site of the Mercat Cross and, of course, the main markets of old Perth, is the Guildhall. It was built originally in 1722, and replaced in 1906 by local architect AG Heiton, and served until 1986 as the headquarters of the Guildry Incorporation (see Chapter 19). It is now in commercial use. On the ground floor are two arched shop fronts, between which is a gilded medallion noting the date of the original building and that of its replacement. The arches support a tall first floor with massive windows into the original Guildhall. Above the middle window are carved figures, by HH Martyn, representing Industry and Commerce supporting

### James Connolly

The original Guildhall links Perth to the Irish Easter Rising. In 1890 James Connolly, the Edinburgh-born son of Irish parents, married Lily Reynolds, an employee of the Guildry, who resided in the Guildhall. The ceremony took place in the St John the Baptist Roman Catholic Church in Melville Street. Later Connolly became one of the most effective and inspirational of the leaders during the 1916 Easter Rising. His execution by firing squad, although so severely wounded he could not stand unaided, contributed greatly to the bitterness against the English in Ireland.

the coat of arms of Perth, and above
that a crown.

## Public Art

At the beginning of the pedestrianised
section of the High Street is the
lifesize bronze of the barefoot Fair
Maid of Perth, sitting on a bench
with a book on her lap (see Chapter
16). Farther up the street, at its
junction with King Edward Street, is
the *Soutar Ring*, an enigmatic bronze
by David Annand (1992). It consists
of a lifesize, blindfolded slave and his
master encircled by an aluminium
ring. On the ring are engraved the
words of William Soutar's poem,
'Nae Day Sae Dark'.

> Nae day sae dark, nae wud sae
> bare;
> Nae grund sae stour wi stane;
> But licht comes through, a sang is
> there;
> A glint o' grass is green.

Gilded plaque between the
two shop fronts of the
Guildhall.

The Fair Maid of Perth,
barefoot, sitting in the High
Street with a book, perhaps
Scott's novel, on her lap.
MAP1·P9

The Soutar Ring. Soutar's
poem, 'Nae Day Sae Dark',
is engraved on the ring.
MAP1·N9

Fish mosaic near Kirkgate.
MAP1·P9

### William Soutar 1898-1943

Perth's William Soutar is one of Scotland's greatest modern poets and finest diarists. He was an able scholar and promising athlete, and enlisted in the Royal Navy in 1917. However, he became progressively crippled and eventually bed ridden by Ankylosing Spondylitis, and died aged only 45. His autobiography is encapsulated in a poem, 'The Earth', part of which has been incised by Gillian Forbes on one of the pillars in the Tay Street floodwall: 'Into a bed, Into a room, Out of the garden, Into a town, And to a country, and up and down.'

A contemporary and friend of Christopher Grieve (Hugh MacDiarmid), and interested in the renaissance of the Scots language that was happening in the 1930s, Soutar was convinced of the importance of the Scots language as a means of expression by Scots people. His poetry is often quoted in relation to Perth, in particular in books and on monuments. He was particularly keen that children should speak Scots, and wrote many short bairn-rhymes in the language. One such is, 'Aince Upon a Day'. The two verses of this poem are inscribed on two pillars in the southern section of the floodwall.

'Aince Upon a Day':

> Aince upon a day my mither said to me,
> Dinna cleip and dinnae rype,
> And dinna tell a lee.
> For gin ye cleip a craw will name ye,
> And if ye rype a daw will shame ye,
> And a snail will heeze its hornies out,
> And hike them round and round about,
> Gin ye tell a lee.

> Aince upon a day, as I walkit a' my lane,
> I met a daw, and mony a craw, and a snail
>     upon a stane.
> Up gaed the daw and didna shame me,
> Up gaed ilk craw and didna name me,
> But the wee snail heez'd its hornies out
> And hiked them round and round about,
> And – goggled at me.

He was also an assiduous and entertaining diarist, recording in particular his innermost feelings as his health deteriorated and he approached death. He spent his last 13 years bedridden at his parents' home at 27 Wilson Street, Perth.

This house, and its contents, in particular the book-lined bedroom, which looks out to the garden, remains as it was when Soutar died. His parents left it to Perth Council and for some time it was used for literary events and writers' groups, and as a house for the Council's 'Writer in Residence'. Currently, however, it is empty and its future is uncertain.

*Top*:
Tay Street Pillar: *The Earth*. Part of an autobiographical poem by William Soutar. 'Into a bed, Into a room, Out of the garden, Into a town, And to a country, and up and down'.

*Middle*:
Tay Street Pilllar. 'Aince Upon a Day', verse 1, by William Soutar.

*Left*:
Tay Street Pillar. 'Aince Upon a Day', verse 2, by William Soutar.

*Right*:
Soutar's house at 27 Wilson Street.
MAP 2 · F2

## High Street: King Edward Street to Methven Street

On the south side of the High Street is one of the entrances to the St John's Centre, and opposite it, the entrance to Perth Theatre, with its canopy projecting into the street (see Chapter 10).

The pedestrianised area of the High Street ends at the junction with Kinnoull Street and Scott Street, and here the street becomes narrower with one-way traffic. On the north side is an unnamed pend with a right of way through to the North Church and Mill Street. The crossroad with Methven Street is the site of the Turret Brig Port, with its associated bridge over the Lade. This was one of the main gates in the city wall, Methven Street itself was built along the line of the wall, adjacent to the Lade which is now completely covered.

## South Street

South Street was variously called 'Soo Gait', or 'South High Gait', and also, because of its weekly shoe market, 'Shoe Gait'. Whatever its name, it was, and remains, the second most important thoroughfare in Perth. It begins in some style between two classical Victorian buildings, the Sheriff Court House and the Fiscal's House on Tay Street, and includes some of the oldest buildings in Perth. Among these are Deuchar's antiques shop, Fountain Close and the Salutation Hotel, which are described in Chapter 6.

There are a number of fine buildings on South Street, but they are less pretentious than those in the High Street, with fewer of the important national chain stores, and fewer prestigious offices. There are, however, some interesting vernacular survivals from the 19th century. Furthermore, it is important as a residential street and also as one of Perth's main shopping streets with many independent retailers.

## Princes Street Corner to King Edward Street

Next to the Salutation Hotel on the corner of Princes Street is another of Perth's extravagant former banks. It was built in 1856 in palazzo style, by David Rhind, who also designed the Lakeland building in St John Street (see Chapter 8). The windows of the ground floor are round-arched, the keystone of each arch being carved with a bearded face. It is now an authentic, and very successful French brasserie, Pig'Halle.

Princes Street itself leads from South Street to the South Inch, where it meets Edinburgh Road. It was constructed in the late 18th century to accommodate the stagecoach traffic into Perth. Now, in the 21st century, retail outlets, cafés and some industrial units are spreading along the street, but in general this large area of Perth, to the south of South Street, is residential.

The broad, elegant block opposite, the junction with Princes Street was built as the City Hotel in 1824. It tapped into the market for travellers arriving by river at the nearby harbour and by coach from Edinburgh. Later, the building was

Entrance to Perth Theatre from the High Street.
MAP1 · M10

Unnamed pend leading from the High Street to the North Church and Mill Street.
MAP1 · L9

Arched window of Pig'Halle restaurant.
MAP1 · P7

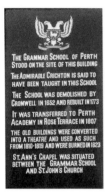

THE GRAMMAR SCHOOL OF PERTH
STOOD ON THE SITE OF THIS BUILDING

THE ADMIRABLE CRICHTON IS SAID TO
HAVE BEEN TAUGHT IN THIS SCHOOL

THE SCHOOL WAS DEMOLISHED BY
CROMWELL IN 1652 AND REBUILT IN 1773

IT WAS TRANSFERRED TO PERTH
ACADEMY IN ROSE TERRACE IN 1807

THE OLD BUILDINGS WERE CONVERTED
INTO A THEATRE AND USED AS SUCH
FROM 1810-1819 AND WERE BURNED IN 1823

ST. ANN'S CHAPEL WAS SITUATED
BETWEEN THE GRAMMAR SCHOOL
AND ST. JOHN'S CHURCH

occupied by Perth Grammar School,
but now the ground floor is a shop
and the upper floors are residential.
The panel in the central window of
the second floor records the history
of the site. When the midday sun
shines down Princes Street, it makes
a fine termination to the street, with
the spire and golden cockerel weather
vane of St John's Kirk rising above it.
The building encloses the entrance to
St Ann's Lane, another of the 'Kirk
Vennels'. It led past St Ann's chapel,
hospital and graveyard, and
connected South Street to the Kirk
precinct. A little further up South
Street is Fleshers Vennel.

On the south side of the street are
three more mediaeval vennels
connecting South Street to Canal

Princes Street Corner, with
the steeple of St John's Kirk
behind.

**The Flesher Incorporation** was a strong guild, which owned much property in this part of the town. Opposite Fleshers' Vennel the guild's insignia can be seen carved above the first floor window of the red sandstone building, which stands on the site of the Fleshers' mediaeval Guild Hall. Modern street bollards in the area are decorated with ox heads.

*Top*:
The insignia of the Fleshers' Guild opposite the entrance to Fleshers Vennel.

Modern street bollard in Fleshers Vennel.

Street: Cow Vennel, Ropemakers Close, and Horners Lane. Cow Vennel was the route from the pasture on the South Inch, via Fleshers' Vennel to the Fleshmarket in front of the Kirk.

The eastern corner of South Street and King Edward Street is occupied by the Salvation Army's Perth Headquarters, consisting of offices and a shop (on King Edward Street), and an Edwardian hall, built of red sandstone in 1904. Opposite, on the ground floor of an impressive corner block is the Auld Hoose tavern, an appropriate foil for the Sally Army. Further up the street is the South Street entrance to the St John's Centre.

COW VENNEL

Modern street sign for a mediaeval thoroughfare.
MAP 1 · O7

Salvation Army headquarters building.
MAP 1 · N7

*An Seann Taigh*, The Auld Hoose Tavern. Corner King Edward Street and South Street.
MAP 1 · O7

## South Street: King Edward Street to South Methven Street

Much of this part of South Street and the vennels leading from it is residential. While the 20th century

'An Seann Taigh', the Gaelic rendering of 'The Auld Hoose', features prominently above those windows of the pub that face King Edward Street. The Gaelic name was first used when Perth hosted the Gaelic Mòd in 2004 in the City Hall just a few yards away – apparently with good commercial effect!

In very general terms, the corner sites on Perth's major streets are occupied by prestigious Victorian or Edwardian buildings, while the terraces in between are mixed with many poorer quality buildings and some 20th century replacements.

Where South Street crosses Scott Street and South Methven Street there are substantial late Victorian/ Edwardian sandstone corner buildings of four stories, several of them topped at the corners with architectural features. At South Methven Street, for example, a copper dome shaped like a German soldier's helmet, with a weather vane on top, looks across South Street to a short tower, with portholes and spire, above the Dickens pub.

South Street/Canal Crescent corner.
MAP 1 · K7

# New Streets in Perth

By the end of the 18th century, there was serious congestion and much squalor in the centre of Perth. Over the next century this problem was addressed by widening Ritten Row (and renaming it St John Street), laying out Methven Street (North and South) along the line of the city wall between Atholl Street and Canal Street (see Chapter 14) and building two completely new streets. These were King Edward Street, linking the precinct of St John's Kirk with the High Street and South Street, and Kinnoull Street, parallel to Methven Street. These streets form the basic street pattern of central Perth today, with many of the old vennels, pends and closes still existing, and providing valuable 'permeability' to the city centre.

architecture is less interesting, the residents bring a vibrancy to the streets that is important in any city. They are also, doubtless, among the regular customers of the local Tesco Metro, which takes up a substantial plot between South Street and Canal Street.

South Street/South Methven Street corner.
MAP 1 · K7

## Kinnoull Street and Scott Street, along with North and South Methven Streets and King Street

These streets are, in fact, two parallel streets running from Atholl Street in the north, crossing Mill Street, the High Street, South Street, and Canal Street to the South Inch. The buildings, especially in the central sections, are in general more homogeneous than those in the High Street and South Street. They are elegant, late Victorian and Edwardian, three- or four-storey terraces, designed and built as shops on the ground floor and residential above – and to a large extent, that purpose has survived. This is where many of Perth's independent retailers are located.

Most of the shop fronts have been modernised, some with little taste, but a few still illustrate the classical

Victorian/Edwardian requirement for the maximum amount of natural light – tall windows, often of curved glass, with slender supporting cast iron columns. The lobby was often tiled with geometric patterns or the name of the shop. Latterly, Art Nouveau decoration and elements of

Four-storey residential tenements with shops below on Scott Street.

Three-storey Edwardian terrace of shops in South Methven Street.

No. 25 Scott Street. One of the best preserved Edwardian shop fronts.

Tiled doorway to No. 25
Scott Street.
MAP 1 · L8

Art Nouveau carved
architectural details on
the doorway to St John's
Centre, Scott Street.
MAP 1 · I8

the Arts and Crafts movement
were incorporated into the designs.
The overall homogeneity of this area
can be ascribed, partly at least, to the
fact that the principal architects
involved came from a limited number
of local firms.

# CHAPTER EIGHT

# The City Centre

## St John's Kirk of Perth, and the Surrounding Streets

St John's Kirk was built on a low mound on the west bank of the river. It was, and remains at the very centre of the City of Perth, and it dominated the mediaeval town that developed around it. The houses, businesses and markets that grew up in its shadow were arranged in streets, lanes and spaces that are still recognisable today.

## St John Street

A short walk down the High Street from the promontory past the Watergate leads to St John Street on the left. Originally it was one of the narrow 'Kirk Vennels', linking the Kirk precincts to the High Street, Watergate and South Street. It was called 'Ritten' or 'Rotten Row', a corruption of the words 'Routine Row', which referred to the processional route to the Burgh Kirk used during the many religious festivals and processions that happened in pre-Reformation Scotland.

However, the mediaeval buildings were demolished in 1801 and the street widened, enabling many elegant buildings to be constructed and opening up the access to the High Kirk. Along with St John's Place and King Edward Street, it was

pedestrianised in 2004, and the lamp standards embellished with modern copper art works by David Wilson. It is now an important shopping street, with a number of the independent locally owned retailers, for which Perth is so famous (see Chapter 17).

Opposite the gable end of St John's Kirk, between Baxters Vennel

Copper public art on lamp post in St John Street.
MAP 1 · P9

81

**McEwens department store** is perhaps the only independent department store left in Scotland. To climb the main staircase in McEwen's is to experience an old listed building founded on silt, and very slowly sinking unevenly into it. The store itself, and especially the second floor café, has a formidable reputation. Many patrons from far and wide visit regularly to do some shopping, and partake of morning coffee, lunch, or afternoon tea.

McEwen's department store.

*Below left*:
Venetian window in St John Street.

Former Bank of Scotland headquarters, now Lakeland.

*Right*:
Elaborate coffered plaster ceiling in Lakeland.

and Oliphants Vennel is the former Headquarters first of the Central Bank of Scotland, and then the Bank of Scotland. This building, which is now occupied by Lakeland, is a three-storey exuberant Italian Renaissance palazzo, with an expensively detailed exterior and magnificent plaster ceilings inside. Clearly the architect, David Rhind, and his client were determined to make a bold statement about the importance of the bank to the businessmen of Perth.

Two other buildings, on the west side of the street, are worth looking at. Nos 3–5 St John Street, occupied now by White Stuff, was also once the Perth headquarters of the Bank of Scotland. It too is a palazzo style building with prestigious pillars on the ground floor, and a cast iron balcony outside the first floor windows. Next door, Austin Reed has a magnificent Venetian window looking onto the street. Inside the oval Georgian stairway to the first floor is capped by a cupola, and has suffered from the same subsidence as the stairway in McEwens.

### 'Little Willie' – the Abernethy Pearl

Freshwater pearls taken from the mussels that thrive in the fast-flowing rivers and streams of Scotland have long been treasured. Pearls, along with gold, underpinned the Roman monetary system, and control of their source was one of four reasons given by Julius Caesar for invading Britain in 55 BC. Their popularity continued in mediaeval times when they were much used in jewellery by, among others, Mary Queen of Scots and Queen Elizabeth of England. Sixty-eight Scottish pearls were mounted on the Scottish crown when it was refashioned for James V in 1540.

In 1967 an exceptional pearl was discovered in the Tay by professional pearl fisherman William Abernethy, and was named after him. Its combination of qualities makes it one of the most perfect freshwater pearls ever to be discovered, not only in Scotland, but perhaps in the whole world. It is perfectly spherical, 12.5mm in diameter and weighs 44 grains. It is free of blemishes, white in colour with a pink overtone, and a striking lustre. It is owned by Mrs Rennie of Cairncross, in St John Street, the local independent jeweller which, for many decades, has purchased almost all of the legally fished Scottish pearls and incorporated them in beautiful rings, brooches and ear rings. 'Little Willie' is on permanent display in the shop.

Sadly, unlicensed over-exploitation of the mussel stocks led to a complete ban on pearl fishing in 1998, and severe restrictions on the sale of all (including second-hand) Scottish freshwater pearls. Cairncross is the only licensed retail shop.

A sculpture on one of the pillars in the Tay Street floodwall, showing an opened mussel shell with a pearl inside, commemorates pearl fishing in the Tay. The legend on the pillar, *Ecce Tiber* ('Behold the Tiber') refers to the account in *The Fair Maid of Perth* of the exclamation by a Roman centurion on first viewing the Tay as he came over the pass in the Ochil Hills. Scott notes that the Tiber in Rome is nothing like as mighty a river as the Tay.

'Little Willie', and the mussel shell in which it was found.

Cairncross, St John Street, purveyor of Tay pearls.

Tay Street Pillar. A pearl mussel, with a pearl inside.

St John's Place from the Kirk
tower. Perth's café culture.

St John's Kirk from the
south-west.
MAP1·O8

Floor-plan of St John's Kirk.

# St John's Place

St John Street opens out into
St John's Place, the pedestrianised
precinct that surrounds St John's
Kirk, and the City Hall. The many
cafés and pubs in this area have risen
to the Council's challenge to develop
a continental 'café culture' in Perth,
with cuisine from several European
countries, and tables and chairs
spilling out onto the wide pavements.

## St John's Kirk of Perth

The first historical reference to a
church in Perth dedicated to St John
the Baptist was in court documents
dated 1126–1128 in which King
David I decreed that the teinds
(revenue including tithes on
agricultural land) normally due to St
John's should be paid to Dunfermline
Abbey, which then assumed
responsibility for the maintenance of
the Kirk and the provision of clergy.
However, there is archaeological
evidence of a church on this site three
centuries earlier.

As befitted the importance of the
Burgh Kirk of the capital of Scotland,
the heart of King Alexander III was
buried here in 1286, following his
untimely death on the cliffs at
Kinghorn in Fife, which precipitated
Scotland into the Wars of
Independence. King Robert the
Bruce, the ultimate victor of that
conflict, is among the many Scottish
monarchs who contributed to the

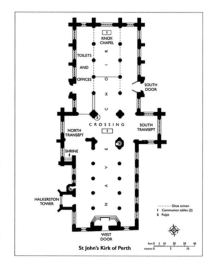

St John's Kirk of Perth

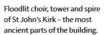

**St Johnstoun**

In many early documents, especially in those of the 16th century, the city is referred to by its alternative moniker, 'St Johnstoun' (St John's town), and the symbol of St John the Baptist – the lamb carrying a staff and banner – featured on the heraldic shield of the City of Perth from mediaeval times until 1975.

construction or alteration of St John's. It is Perth's oldest surviving building, and is the centrepiece of Perth's built environment.

In the mid-15th century, Perth's growing importance and wealth stimulated the staged reconstruction of the church. The choir was probably complete by 1448, when the high altar was consecrated, and the transepts and crossing followed soon after. In the 1490s King James IV funded the construction of the nave, and it is known for certain that the tower and spire were completed before 1511, because in that year the contract for the tower of Aberdeen's St Machar's Cathedral cited St John's as a model to copy – an indication of its architectural importance.

On 11 May 1559, St John's was the scene of a pivotal event in Scotland's history. War clouds were looming between the Catholic Queen Regent, Mary of Guise (mother of Mary Queen of Scots), and an increasingly Protestant people, backed in Perth by their Burgh Council. The Queen had summoned all Protestant preachers to appear before her in Stirling. Meantime, the Protestant lords had assembled an (unarmed) army of nobles and lords, who had arrived in Perth. At that critical moment, John Knox returned to Scotland from Switzerland. When the preachers did not show up in Stirling, the Queen declared them all to be rebels, which enraged the people of Perth. At this tense juncture Knox preached his sermon against idolatry in St John's Kirk. The congregation was so inflamed that they stripped the Kirk of its ornaments and then stormed out of the church, sacking Perth's wealthy religious houses, and setting alight the Scottish Reformation.

Following the Reformation, St John's, like many other Scottish churches, fell into disrepair. The Crown had expropriated much of the wealth that had previously maintained religious establishments, and the fledgling Reformed Church struggled to pay its ministers, repair the ravages of the Reformation and attend to ordinary maintenance. Furthermore, in the new Presbyterian

order, large congregations were
divided into smaller units that could
be managed by a single parish
minister. This in turn led to large
church buildings being divided by
walls into two, or even three separate
churches. And so, at the end of the
16th century, the three western bays
of St John's were walled off to form a
separate 'West Kirk', with its own
minister, and later two further
churches were created from the
transepts and choir.

## Restoration by Sir Robert Lorimer

During the 19th century, opinion
about the church buildings gradually
changed and the people of Perth
came to appreciate that their High
Kirk, although severely mutilated,
was in its basic structure still largely
intact, including in particular the
choir, with its original ceiling and roof.

1  *A History of St
John's Kirk of Perth*
by Richard
Fawcett. Published
by The Friends of
St John's Kirk of
Perth, 1967.

Some work was done in the 1820s and
in the 1890s, but it was not until the
First World War that a committee was
established to restore the building to a
single church, and to incorporate
within it a memorial to the men and
women of Perth and Perthshire who
had lost their lives in that conflict. Sir
Robert Lorimer was engaged as the
architect, and it is his sensitive
restoration that revealed the 15th
century building that we see today.

The church is cruciform, built of
smooth ashlar, and is approximately
the same size and proportions as the
other important late mediaeval burgh
churches in Scotland (St Giles' in
Edinburgh, St Michael's in
Linlithgow, and St Mary's in
Haddington). The late Richard
Fawcett in his book *A History of St
John's Kirk of Perth* states: 'Few
churches can now give such a
complete impression of the mediaeval
appearance of a great Scottish burgh
church as St John's, and it is therefore
a particularly precious survival.'[1]

The choir is the most original
(ie 15th century) part of the church.
The arches separating the choir from
the side aisles rise to about two thirds
of the height to the roof, above which
are the clerestory windows, which
allow light to flood in. The roof of
the choir, which is one of Scotland's

The Nave of St John's Kirk.
© Angus Findlay Photography.

*Right*:
Painted panel in the roof of the nave, depicting Jesus before Pontius Pilate.

Halkerston Tower.

The communion table with its embroidered cloth and colourful candlesticks.
© Louis Flood.

few surviving major mediaeval oak tie-beam roofs, was exposed and restored by Lorimer. In 1970 the section of the choir beneath the great east window, which in mediaeval times contained the high altar, was converted into a separate chapel, as a memorial to the members of the congregation who died in the Second World War, and named after John Knox.

The nave, largely rebuilt by Lorimer, lacks the clerestory windows of the choir and has a barrel ceiling of fumed oak also by Lorimer, decorated with coloured panels depicting the life of Christ. On the north side of the nave is the Halkerston Tower, which was the entrance to the church for the laity in the 15th century. Internally, it has a ribbed vault dating from the late 15th century, but externally it has been very much altered.

The communion table is plain, but covered by a cloth which commemorates the life and work of Alastair Cairncross, who was for many years the chairman of the Friends of St John's Kirk of Perth. The colourful candlesticks on the communion table were the gift of

Perth & Kinross District Council in 1993 to celebrate the 750th anniversary of the Kirk's consecration.

The main entrance to the Kirk, as for all similar churches, was through the great west door. Nick Crane, in his television documentary about Perth (Towns series, 2011) noted how the ground level around St John's Kirk had become so raised due to centuries of burials that the proportions of the west door of the church were distorted – it was so much shorter than it should be. He commented that 'the congregation of the dead were impeding the access to the church by the congregation of the living'! There are plans to lower the level of the street outside the door, and so to restore the proportions of the doorway, and ease the access to the Kirk.

A more serious distortion to the Kirk's fabric was the shortening of the north transept in 1823 to improve traffic flow in St John's Place!

The pews in the north transept were for members of the Incorporated Guilds of Perth. On the sides of these pews are engraved the crests of Perth's ancient guilds, while on the front of the first pew is the Coat of Arms of Perth & Kinross District Council (see below). On ceremonial occasions, these pews are now used by the members of the Perth Society of High Constables. A splendid 15th century Flemish brass candelabrum hangs in this transept, close to the shrine. It is probably the only one of its type in Scotland and features the Virgin and Child set in a sunburst at its apex. There are 12

Carving on a pew in the north transept. Hammermen, 'By Hammer and hand all arts do stand'.

The west door of St John's. Much shorter than it should be. Ram's head bollard in front.

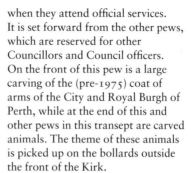

when they attend official services. It is set forward from the other pews, which are reserved for other Councillors and Council officers. On the front of this pew is a large carving of the (pre-1975) coat of arms of the City and Royal Burgh of Perth, while at the end of this and other pews in this transept are carved animals. The theme of these animals is picked up on the bollards outside the front of the Kirk.

On the wall of the south transept is a colourful carved wooden panel dating from the 18th century featuring the insignia of the Wrights' Incorporation. It was originally in the East Kirk.

## Perth's War Memorial

The north transept of the restored Kirk contains the official memorial to the men and women of Perth and Perthshire who gave their lives in the First World War. It is the apogee of Lorimer's work on St John's, and is described in Chapter 18, Perth's War Memorials.

branches representing the 12 apostles. It is not electrified.

The south transept contains the pew reserved for the Provost and important dignitaries of the city

## Tower and Spire

The square central tower is supported by four massive pillars at the corners of the crossing. The ceiling of the crossing is vaulted, with

*Top left*:
The 15th century candelabrum.

Coat of arms of the (pre-1975) City and Royal Burgh of Perth on Provost's pew.

*Top right*:
Crouching ape on the end of the Provost's pew.

Modern bollard with a lion's head.

*Left*:
Carved wooden panel with the insignia of the Wrights' Incorporation.

Clockwise:
Tay Street pillar, depicting the coat of arms of Perth, Ontario, Perth's twin city in Canada.

Coat of arms carved on the external wall of the Old Council Chambers.

Coat of arms of Perth & Kinross District Council, on the first pew in the north transept.

### Coat of Arms of the City and Royal Burgh of Perth

John the Baptist is traditionally associated with a lamb. This derives from the verse in the Bible, (John, 1:29) which records that when John the Baptist saw Jesus approaching he said, 'Behold the Lamb of God'. The lamb is always depicted carrying a staff and a banner. In the case of the City and Royal Burgh of Perth the coat of arms consisted of a red shield with a lamb carrying a staff and a banner featuring a Saltire, all within a double tressure, signifying Royal favour. The motto was, *Pro Rege, Lege, et Grege*, (For the King, the Law and the People).

The shield is supported by a double-headed eagle in gold. The double-headed eagle is the most ancient heraldic symbol in the world, originating in the Sumerian city of Lagash in modern Iraq, some 4,000 years BC, and known to the kings of the time as the Storm Bird. It was used throughout ancient times, and ultimately brought to the West during the Crusades. Charlemagne first made used of it in 802 AD, when he united the Frankish Empire (most of modern France, Germany and Austria) with Italy to form the Holy Roman Empire. The two heads signified the two kingdoms under his rule. How the eagle came to Perth is lost in time, but it may be related to the imagined Roman origins of Perth, and confusion between the military empire of the City of Rome and the Holy Roman Empire of Charlemagne! It first appeared on the official seals of Perth in about 1673, and is carved on the exterior wall of the Old Council Chambers, facing the High Street, at first floor level.

It is still used by a number of organisations, including St Johnstone Football Club, and the Perth and District Pipe Band (founded in 1893), and (without the supporting eagle) by the town of Perth in Ontario, Canada – twinned with Perth in 2001.

### Coat of Arms of Perth & Kinross District Council

In the reorganisation of local government in 1975, Tayside Region, based in Dundee, took over many of the functions of the Perth's Royal Burgh Council, along with those of the County Councils of Perth, Kinross, and Angus, and of the many Burgh Councils. The remaining functions were administered by Perth & Kinross District Council, but were not considered sufficiently important to justify Perth's

city status, nor the retention of the Lord Provostship, which was abolished.

The coat of arms of the District Council reflected its three constituent elements. The rampant lion was taken from the coat of arms of Perth County. It is the symbol of King William I, the Lion of Scotland, who gave Perth its Royal Charter in 1210. It is shown brandishing a scimitar ready to defend its country. Emblasoned on the breast of the lion was a depiction of Loch Leven Castle, which had previously featured on the coat of arms of Kinross County Council. The double-headed eagle was Perth's contribution to the coat of arms.

However, that did not happen automatically. The Court of the Lord Lyon had sought to exclude the eagle bearer because it considered the newly created District Council was not sufficiently important to justify such a proud emblem. However, after a strong case was made by councillors and officials from Perth, it was allowed as a special case, 'To mark the fact that the City of Perth was a former capital of Scotland and took precedence over all Scottish burghs, except Edinburgh' (RM Urquhart, Scottish Civic Heraldry, 1979).

A coronet, appropriate for a District Council, encircles the necks of the eagle. On it are eight thistle heads (five visible). The motto was changed to, *Pro Lege et Libertate* (For Law and Liberty).

A startling difference between the two coats of arms is that the eagle in the Royal Burgh of Perth arms is golden (with fearsome red beaks and claws), while in the arms of the District Council (and later of the Perth & Kinross Council) it is black, but with the same red beak, feet and claws. No explanation for the change has been forthcoming. What is possible is that the Lord Lyon, perhaps inadvertently, chose black, which is the usual colour for such eagle bearers in European heraldry, and indeed in Scotland for the town of Lanark. Meanwhile the officials and councillors from Perth were so happy to have succeeded in retaining their eagle that they did not quibble about its colour!

## Coat of Arms of Perth & Kinross Council (1996)

In the reorganisation of 1996, Tayside Region was abolished and full powers were restored to Perth. The new Council chose to simplify the name to Perth & Kinross Council. The coat of arms changed little, differing from that of the District Council only in the coronet. This now has eight spikes (five visible), between the eight thistles (four visible). This is appropriate in heraldic terms for an Area Council. The motto remains *Pro Lege et Libertate*.

The coat of arms of Perth & Kinross Council, established 1996.

Carved wooden boss filling the hole through which bells were lifted into the tower.

Close-up of the names. Also inscribed are the names of the plumber and carpenter.

a large space in the centre to permit the hoisting of bells into the tower. This is filled by a carved wooden boss depicting Perth's symbol – the Lamb of God with the staff and banner. However, the banner carried by the Lamb features the Cross of St George, rather than the Saltire! In the centre of the crossing, is the communion table, and within the first arch of the nave a large wooden cross hangs from 15th century iron hooks in the roof.

The eight-sided, splay-footed broach spire is covered in ribbed lead sheeting. This sheeting was blown down in a gale in 1767 and replaced by the Burgh Council. On the west face of the spire is inscribed the names of the members of the Burgh Council who authorised the work, along with the names of the plumber and carpenter who carried it out. The spire has been a landmark over Perth

for 500 years, and rises from the tower to a golden cockerel weather vane 155 feet above the pavement. On its north face is a unique open bartizan belfry or lucarne-bellcote, which houses 13 of Perth's collection of bells.

## The Bells

*St Johnstoun's bells ring bonnie,*
*And awaken echoes many.*
                                    OLD SONG

In the lower right-hand corner of the Gow window in the south aisle is a picture of King David the psalmist playing a set of bells with hammers. It provides a fitting start to the discussion of the largest collection of bells in the British Isles.

From St John's tower the 'Bells of Perth' have rung out over the centuries, marking great state occasions, telling the time and calling parishioners to worship. There are 63

The steeple from the west, showing the names of the Members of the Burgh Council in post when the lead was renewed in 1767.

bells, eight of which were cast before the Reformation, and would have been heard by John Knox. The carillon, which is played regularly, consists of 35 of these bells. They include the largest bell in the collection, the early 16th-century 'Bourdon' (the Johannes Baptista), which is the keynote bell, with a further 34 bells cast in 1935. This modern carillon was promoted by Mr Melville Gray of Bowerswell House and installed at a cost of £3,000, paid for by many donors, including, notably, Melville Gray himself. Some of the donors chose to have a bell inscribed with the name of a family member killed in the Great War. The inscription round the top of the 'Bourdon' reads:

Detail from the Gow window. King David the psalmist, playing the bells with hammers.

The 'Bourdon,' cast in 1506, and mounted on a wheel.

Dr Cassells, carillonneur at St John's, playing the clavier in the tower.

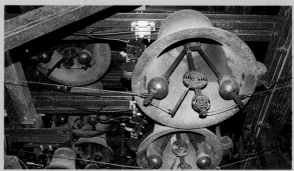

This bell has four hammers. An electronic one (black) on the left, a clapper for the clavier, another for a previous automatic player, and a hammer for the clock chimes.

**Campanology in Scotland** follows the North European tradition, and is quite different from the norm in England. The bells are fixed, and tunes are played on them using a clavier, or keyboard, like an organ. This has substantial keys and pedals, each connected by a wire tracker to a clapper which strikes the bell. The carillonneur plays the bells by hitting the keys with his fists. All types of music can be played, including hymn tunes, popular melodies and music composed especially for bells.

The Norie-Miller Bell.

Close-up of the inscription round the top of the Bourdon, with the small image of John the Baptist.

*Right*:
Thirteen bells in the Bartizan Belfry.

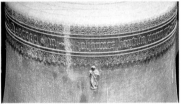

'*Johannes Baptista Vocor Ego*
*Vox Clamantis in Deserto*
*Mechlin Petrus Waghevens Me Fo'*
    *mavit*
*Sit Benedictus Qui Cuncta Creavit.*
    *M CCCCC VI'*

'(*John the Baptist I am called*
'*The voice of one crying in the*
    *wilderness.*
*Peter Weghevens made me at Mechlin*
    [*in Flanders*]
*Let Him be blest who created all*
    *things. 1506*)'

Beneath the inscription is a small image of John the Baptist.

The bartizan belfry on the north side of the spire, the only such belfry in Scotland, houses 13 bells. They were played regularly until the modern carillon was installed in 1935, but have been silent since. The largest of these, the 'Maria', is the oldest of all the bells, and has an unusual elongated shape. It was probably cast in England in the early 14th century, around 200 years before the 'Bourdon'. The inscription reads:

*Ave Maria Gracia Plena Dominus*
    *Tecum.*
(*Hail Mary, full of Grace, the Lord is*
    *with thee*).

The remaining 15 bells can be seen in the south aisle of the choir, hanging in an iron frame. They include six pre-Reformation bells. The largest of these is the 'Agnus Dei', and bears the inscription:

*ECCE AGNUS DEI*
(*Behold the Lamb of God*).

Recent research suggests it was cast in Scotland in about 1340, around 160 years before the 'Bourdon', and before the tower was built. It probably came from a previous church on this site. The other five pre-Reformation bells are a tuned set cast in Mechlin in 1526. These bells, with three others, form an octave and can be played in the church using a wooden hammer similar to that used by King David as depicted in the Gow window.

The modern carillon is played on Sunday mornings, and there are regular recitals during the year. In 2013 an electronic mechanism was installed, which enables the bells to be played from a keyboard adjacent to the organ console.

## The Town Clock

As well as housing the bells, the tower also has the town clock. The present mechanism was presented to the city of Perth by Andrew Graham, a former Lord Provost in 1879 and chimes the hours and Guildford quarters. However, it was not the first clock. The earliest references to the clock are in a town minute for 'mending and repairing the nock (sic)' in 1607, and in the 16th century there was a saying in the city that, 'The Sun and Moon may gang wrang, but the clock of St Johnstoun canna gang wrang'. This refers to the first clock face, which indicated day and night and the lunar phases with the sun and the moon, as do some old grandfather clocks.

Following an accident when the clock was over-wound and the weight fell onto the roof of the crossing (fortunately doing no more damage then dislodging some plaster), the mechanism was electrified.

## Stained Glass

While St John's has no mediaeval glass, it does have a remarkable collection of stained glass windows by the best Scottish artists of the 20th century. Above the west door is the great west window by Herbert

Carillon of 15 bells mounted in the south transept.

The town clock. 'Presented to The City Of Perth by Andrew Graham Esq. ex-Lord Provost, 1879'.

Detail from the great west window featuring the Nativity, by Herbert Hendrie.

Douglas Strachan's great east window depicting the Crucifixion.

One of two oak cases for the organ pipes, designed by Sir Robert Lorimer.

Hendrie. Its main feature is the Nativity, and this theme is complemented in the great east window, which depicts the crucifixion, by Douglas Strachan. The Black Watch window, the shrine window and the Gow window (above), are referred to elsewhere in this text.

## The Church Organ

The three manual pneumatic action organ, installed in 1926, is housed in two splendid oak cases, designed by Sir Robert Lorimer. It incorporates the 1873 Conacher of Huddersfield instrument, which had served the East Kirk in the building prior to Lorimer's restoration. It was refurbished in 2003, and the action, now electromagnetic, is controlled from a detached oak console, which can be moved and played in almost any part of the building. There are regular recitals by the Director of Music at St John's and visiting organists.

## Modern Refurbishment

Most recently, in 2010–13, £2.75m has been raised and spent to refurbish the interior of the Kirk. Lorimer's wooden chairs have been replaced with more comfortable seating, and the lighting, heating, toilets, office accommodation and electronics brought up to a modern standard. This is not only for the comfort of parishioners on Sunday mornings, but also to facilitate the use of the building as a venue for concerts and other events.

## Other Churches Dedicated to St John the Baptist

There are two other churches in Perth dedicated to St John the Baptist: the Roman Catholic Church in Melville Street, built in 1832, and the Episcopalian Church in Princes Street, built with its 150-foot spire in 1851.

## King Edward Street and the City Hall

By the end of the 19th century Perth's existing City Hall had become quite inadequate, and an ambitious plan to build a new City Hall and a new street linking the Kirk precincts to the High Street and South Street was promoted. Completed in 1902, the street was named, with Royal permission, King Edward Street, after the newly crowned King Edward VII.

The City Hall, a large imposing building, was completed in 1911, and is now B-listed. It occupies the bulk of the space between the Kirk and King Edward Street. By the end of the 20th century, however, it required

huge expenditure to bring it up to modern standards, and even with that would have lacked the 'break-out space' required for conferences and other functions. A decision was taken to build a new Concert Hall, which was completed in 2005, and the old City Hall was closed.

The Council wishes to demolish the Hall and convert the space in front of the Kirk into a continental style city square, suitable for markets and events. This would open up the

The City Hall façade.
MAP 1 · N8

The City Hall from St John's tower.

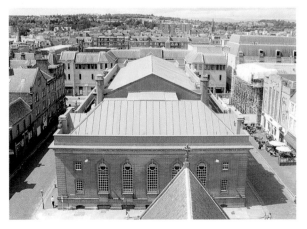

view of the mediaeval church, the jewel in Perth's architectural heritage, which is at present hemmed in by buildings all around, and dwarfed by the City Hall. This proposal, however, has been blocked by Historic Scotland, which has asked for more efforts to be made to find a commercial use for the building. At the time of writing, therefore, the future of the City Hall is very uncertain.

Opposite the front of the City Hall is the main entrance to the St John's Centre, an indoor shopping mall. There is a pedestrian connection through the St John's Centre to the High Street, and also a passageway to Kinnoull Street.

The Centre was opened in 1988 and is about to undergo a major refurbishment.

# Edward VII Memorial

Following the death of the King, a memorial was built in front of the City Hall and unveiled in 1913. A massive octagonal drum, it is Perth's third Mercat Cross. It is said to be a reinterpretation of Perth's 1669 Mercat Cross, on the High Street. Each of the eight sides of the memorial consists of a panel, and above it a roundel. The west-facing panel contains a granite plaque and bronze relief of the bust of the King, and the others have various coats of arms. In the roundels above are the insignia of the guilds that comprise Perth's Guildry Incorporation: Wrights, Glovers, Weavers, Baxters (Bakers), Cordiners (shoemakers),

Aschaffenburg, Perth's twin city in Bavaria, is twice honoured in the St John's Centre. The office complex above the centre is called St Martyn's House after Aschaffenburg's patron saint, and Aschaffenburg's coat of arms (also featuring St Martyn) is displayed above the entrance to the centre from the High Street.

St Martyn's House.

The Aschaffenburg plaque inside the High Street entrance of the St John's Centre.

Hammermen, Fleshers and Tailors. The shaft of the cross is topped by a unicorn holding a shield, and carrying a bronze flagstaff and Saltire.

## Farmers' Market

On the first Saturday of each month, King Edward Street is the site of Perth's famous Farmers' Market, which successfully brings local produce into the city centre. It is enormously popular with the citizens of Perth, and has attracted royal visitors (see Chapter 17).

# CHAPTER NINE

# George Street and Tay Street

BY THE MID-1700S, inter-city travel was causing traffic problems in Perth. Large stagecoaches with four horses could not negotiate the narrow, congested streets, especially the Skinnergate and Watergate. Moreover, plans were being developed to end Perth's 150 years of reliance on ferries, and build a new bridge at the northern end of the city, which would bring more vehicular traffic into Perth from Dundee and the north-east.

And so George Street was planned to bypass the Skinnergate, and connect the new bridge to the High Street and the centre of the city. It was opened in 1771, the same year as the new bridge was completed, and was soon lined with elegant buildings. Exactly a century later, Tay Street was built to enable traffic from Edinburgh and the south to access the city centre and the bridge. It completely obliterated the old harbour and waterfront, but remains today the most recognisable street in Perth.

## George Street

By the standards of the times, George Street was a broad, elegant street that met the requirements of the era. Over the next 50 years, it was built up on either side with many prestigious buildings for banks, fashionable houses, coffee parlours and shops.

Former Perth Bank, by Andrew Heiton Junior.
MAP 1 · P10

Restored Georgian building with traditional Scottish chimneyed gable.
MAP 1 · P11

Many of these buildings are now listed, some of them with characteristic Scottish chimneyed gable ends to the street.

The George Inn, now the Royal George Hotel, was built in 1773 close to the landfall of the Perth Bridge (a portion of the City Wall being demolished in the process). It was at first a modest coaching inn, servicing the travellers to and from Edinburgh, Glasgow, Inverness and Aberdeen. Business prospered, and a number of famous coaches, including 'The Diligence', 'The Caledonian', and 'The Fair Maid' called regularly to change the horses and rest the travellers.

The Inn's fortunes really took off in September 1848, when Queen Victoria and Prince Albert, forced to travel south from Balmoral by road and rail because the royal yacht was stormbound, arrived unexpectedly at

Queen Victoria's royal coat of arms in the lounge of the Royal George Hotel.

Perth Railway Station, and wished to stay the night. Although the hotel staff had only 30 minutes warning, the Queen was well pleased with her stay, and later awarded the inn a Royal Warrant. A large depiction of the Royal Coat of Arms in carved oak wood hangs in the hotel lounge, and two of the bedposts from the Royal Bed have been made into standard lamps. Thereafter the coaching inn moved up in the world to become the Royal George Hotel!

Interestingly, in this crest, the

The red carpet laid out at the Royal George Hotel.
MAP 1 · P11

The Royal bedpost standard light, and Royal Coat of Arms.

streets, with a wide selection of independent retailers, coffee shops, and small craft businesses. Some of these shops, although small, have significant reputations, while others attract attention by using bizarre names.

## Tay Street

In 1833 the first moves were made to develop a new harbour for Perth at Friarton, a mile downstream from the mediaeval quays. While that took time to mature, the city's original harbour along the river frontage was in decline. At the same time there was a need to improve the flow of traffic between the Perth Bridge and the Edinburgh Road. And so, the plans for Tay Street were conceived and building started in 1869. A massive embankment was constructed on top

unicorn is on the left, whereas it is usually on the right. In another Royal Coat of Arms above the reception desk, the lion and the unicorn are correctly positioned. Over the last 200 years, the hotel has been extended and developed continuously, and now also opens on to Tay Street, where there is an award-winning garden.

George Street is now one of Perth's most important shopping

Tay Street: St Matthew's Church to the Fergusson Gallery.

of the gardens, jetties, quays and beaches that lined the riverfront from the Perth Bridge to the South Inch. Tay Street was laid out on top of it – a broad promenade affording a very fine outlook for the buildings that grew up along its west side. It is now very much the public face of Perth – elegant, restrained, proportional, Victorian. It is the view of Perth seen from the bridges and is the subject of countless photographs and paintings. The final stage in the development was the planting of trees along the riverside, in 1881. By 2000 these trees were post mature and were removed, but new trees were planted and have taken well.

## A Walk Down Tay Street – Red (Middle Free) Church to the High Street

In contrast to the architectural hotchpotch of George Street, Tay Street has a pleasing symmetry.

Undoubtedly this is due to the fact that more than three-quarters of the buildings were designed by just two local architectural partnerships – the Heiton family and John Young and his son GPK Young. Four other architects each designed one building – the two churches, the Sheriff Court and one other. The overall effect is of a grand, unified boulevard with a magnificent and constantly changing view of the river, and of the wooded slopes of Kinnoull Hill beyond.

However, starting the walk from the Perth Bridge, the first two buildings do not have that 'Tay Street feel' about them, and do not contribute to the symmetry mentioned above. Then, set lower down and back from the street is the rear entrance of the Royal George Hotel, with its huge new conservatory stretching the whole width of the building, providing guests with a stunning view of the river and bridge.

## The Red (Middle Free) Church

Scotland's post-Reformation ecclesiastical history featured sequential splits in the Reformed Church, resulting in competitive construction of new churches by the new congregations. This has left places like Perth with a surfeit of church buildings, many of which have become redundant. Some have been demolished or converted into housing or business premises, and others have been purchased by the smaller denominations. A few of these buildings are worthy of inclusion in a book such as this, either because of their important position in the city's architectural fabric, or because of the contribution they make to city life. Two of them are on Tay Street – the Red Church, formerly the Middle Free Church, and St Matthew's Church.

The Red Church was designed by Hippolyte Jean Blanc, an Edinburgh

architect of French extraction. He built many churches across Scotland in the Gothic Revival style, with a French accent. It is a large and confident construction, albeit with only a modest fleche rather than a spire or tower. It is built of red sandstone, sourced from Corsiehill, just across the river. A sensitive

The rear entrance of the Royal George Hotel overlooking the River Tay and the outfall of the Lade.

The Red Kirk and its fleche.
MAP 1 · Q11

conversion to housing in 1965 has preserved its architectural integrity, and its contribution to the streetscape.

## Council Chambers – Old and New

The range of buildings, extending all the way from the Red Church round the corner to No. 5 High Street, was designed by Andrew Heiton Junior in continental gothic style. The terrace includes the District Court (now disused), and a pend, behind which was the fire station in the days of horse-drawn fire engines. On the corner and extending up the High Street is a suite of Council offices. On the opposite corner, across the High Street, are the new Council Chambers (see Chapter 7).

## Tay Street: From the High Street to South Street

### The Capital Asset

Lying between the new Council Chambers and St Matthew's Church is another former bank, now one of the Wetherspoon chain of pubs. It is more flamboyant than any of Andrew Heiton Junior's other Tay Street buildings, doubtless because his banking client was insisting on keeping up with the other lavish bank buildings in Perth.

### St Matthew's Church of Scotland

With its 210 foot open spire this, the tallest building in Perth, was designed by the Glasgow architect John Honeyman. It adds tremendous

height and perspective to Tay Street, and to countless paintings and photographs of Perth. Internally, however, the church is quite plain.

**The Capital Asset**

For some years now, on Christmas Eve, carol singing and a watch-night service in The Capital Asset have been conducted by the minister from St Matthew's Church next door.

A former bank, the Capital Asset.
MAP 1 · Q9

The spire of St Matthew's Church dominates Tay Street and Perth's bridges on a cold January morning.

**Wildlife.** Some years ago Peregrine Falcons nested in the spire, and the RSPB set up a viewing station in the courtyard below. More recently the birds have moved to the crags of Kinnoull Hill across the Tay, but they still use the pinnacles of the St Matthew's spire as a feeding station to teach their young how to catch prey – generally pigeons, of which there are plenty. Other wildlife is plentiful on the Tay, in particular, seals, otters and all manner of wildfowl.

A Goosander and ten chicks seen in front of St Matthew's Church.

*Above right:*
The Fiscal's House, now converted to housing.

*Below:*
Gowrie House by John Young. Note the symmetry and the central pend.

Consecrated in 1871, it served for many years as the Black Watch Regimental Kirk, and so was the repository for a number of Regimental colours which are now laid up in the church.

Between St Matthews Church and the Sheriff Court there is a long terrace of offices. The northern half was built in grey ashlar by Andrew Heiton Junior, while the southern half of the terrace was designed by John Young, with a pend in the middle. It is named Gowrie House (see Chapter 6). The separate corner block was built as Fiscal offices for the Sheriff Court, but has been converted to housing.

## Tay Street: South Street to Canal Street

### Sheriff Courthouse

This imposing building, in the classical revival style with a central portico supported by 12 fluted columns, occupies the whole of the plot between South Street and Canal Street. Built on the site of the original Gowrie House, it was the result of a

design competition, the successful architect being Robert Smirke, who also designed the British Museum and the nearby Kinfauns Castle.

## Tay Street: Canal Street to the South Inch

From Canal Street to the Greyfriars Cemetery gate is John Young's symmetrical French Renaissance style terrace, built in 1881. The central block (No. 66) housed the museum of the Perthshire Society of Natural Science, and on the north corner was Perth's Opera House. Opera however was to be short-lived, and in 1892 the Baptist church took over the building and used it until it burned down in 1983. It was replaced by a modern sandstone faced housing development which, while neither pastiche nor modern, generally blends well with its neighbours.

The Sheriff Court House. MAP 1 · Q7

French Renaissance style terrace at Nos. 62–72 Tay Street, with modern housing replacing the fire-destroyed corner building.

cemetery was opened on the site of the Franciscan (Greyfriars) Monastery, behind the buildings on the southern end of Tay Street. Sadly, when Cromwell ransacked the city in 1651, he took away all the headstones to provide building material for his citadel. However,

### Greyfriars Cemetery

As with all other ancient burghs, Perth's dead were buried within the church, or as near to it as possible. In 1580, however, to ease the congestion in the graveyard, a new

### Gowrie House Plaque

Occupying the space of one of the windows of the Sheriff Court House overlooking the Tay is a bronze panel in three sections. The top section is a picture of the original Gowrie House. The central section reads, 'Within gardens bounded by the Tay near this spot stood Gowrie House, noted for the historical event called the Gowrie Conspiracy of 5 August, 1600. Built in 1520. Taken down in 1807'. Below that are the Royal Arms of Scotland on the left and the Arms of the Earls of Gowrie.

Gowrie House plaque on the Sheriff Court House.

during the second half of the 17th
and the 18th centuries, Greyfriars
became the last resting place for most
of the important people of Perth, and
so it has one of the largest and most
important collections of gravestones
in Scotland, and is now A-listed.

The graveyard was restored in
2000, some of the most important
gravestones moved under a shelter to
protect them from the weather. The
main gateway to the cemetery is off
the car park in Canal Street, but a
new entrance was formed on to Tay
Street. The wrought iron gates to this
entrance feature a sunburst, and a
relief of symbols found repeatedly on
grave monuments – the hour glass,
the skull and crossed bones, and
winged souls ascending to heaven.

Beyond the graveyard there is a
modern block of housing and offices
designed to harmonise with the rest
of the late 19th century street and fill
the gap before the railway bridge.
The first of these offices, No. 74, is
the home of the Word Curling
Federation.

## Fergusson Gallery

At the southern end of Tay Street,
beyond the railway bridge, looking
over the South Inch, is the Fergusson
Gallery, which is dedicated to the
works of the Scottish Colourist John
Duncan Fergusson and his lifelong

partner, the dancer and choreographer Margaret Morris.

The museum was originally Perth's waterworks, and was designed in the style of a Greco-Roman temple by Adam Anderson, the Rector of Perth Academy and Professor of Natural Philosophy at St Andrews University. It was built in

1827, over 40 years before Tay Street was laid out. The upper domed rotunda contained the cast iron cistern, and behind it was the pump-house, and steam-fired boiler room with its unusual stone chimney, topped by an urn.

Water was drawn from the Tay, filtered in beds on Moncrieffe Island opposite the waterworks, and then piped across the river to the cistern, before being distributed round the city. The bold motto above the door, *Aquam Igne Aqua Haurio*, can be translated as, 'I draw water by fire and water (steam)'.

Following the construction of new water works, the building was used as a tourist office, but became redundant in 1992. Fortuitously, at

*The Hat with the Pink Scarf,*
by John Duncan Fergusson.
© The Fergusson Gallery, Perth &
Kinross Council.

Outside the gallery is a stylised headless bronze nude statue, *Torse de Femme*. Fergusson was the only one of the Colourist group to experiment with 3D work, and he produced a number of classic female sculptures. Because of the cost of a full-size casting, most of them were made in miniature and advertised as 'available to cast'. The model for this one was sculpted by Fergusson in 1918, and cast for the Perth Gallery in 1994 by Bill Hepworth of the Alyth Art Foundation.

Fergusson's wife, Margaret Morris, was famous in her own right as a dancer and choreographer, and the founder of the Margaret Morris Movement. She died in Glasgow in 1980, and in due course her archive also came to Perth, making a truly exceptional resource for scholars interested in two great talents of the first half of the 20th century.

that time Fergusson's executors (he died in 1961) were looking for a building in Scotland to display the paintings and artefacts from his estate. The two came together in the most imaginative conversion of a Georgian building anywhere in Scotland, resulting in a bright, well-planned gallery. It contains the world's largest collection of paintings by JD Fergusson, including many of his best works, some of which had lain unseen in his studio in Glasgow for 30 years. In addition there are many sketches, photographs and other memorabilia, as well as note books, letters etc.

# CHAPTER TEN

# Mill Street and Perth's Cultural Quarter

Mill Street was an industrial street, with mills lining the northern arm of the Lade, which ran along the outside of the city wall before flowing into the Tay just downstream from the Perth Bridge. The Lade flowed swiftly, providing water and power for many small mills, bleach fields, and other industrial developments. By the middle of the 18th century the city was expanding rapidly, and the area around Mill Street was heavily industrialised, with Pullars of Perth occupying a huge site on its north side. Gradually the Lade was covered over, and now it can be seen only at the Red Brig opposite the Concert Hall.

## Perth Museum and Art Gallery

The street is now undergoing gentrification as it is redeveloped by the Council to become Perth's cultural quarter. To explore this rapidly changing area, begin on the Perth Bridge, and look down towards Mill Street. The dome of the Museum and Art Gallery with its four ionic pillars dominates the view, but the building to the right, with its bow front beneath a Venetian window and pediment, and the adjacent pedimented two-storey extension is the earlier building. Its date is not

View of the Old Post Office and the Marshall Monument from the Perth Bridge.
MAP1·P12

known, but it features on a map dated 1784, 40 years before the museum was built. In the mid-19th century the ground floor of this building was Perth's first Post Office, but for some years now it has operated as a licensed restaurant.

Perth's art collections, its botanical and zoological specimens and its huge range of historical and archaeological artefacts are all now contained in this single building, the Museum and Art Gallery. It stands on the mound leading to the Perth Bridge, near to what is thought to be the site of Perth's castle. Perth is built on a thick layer of silt, washed down by the Tay over many millennia. This has proved to be an excellent preservative for the artefacts and

Museum and Art Gallery from George Street.

remains left by our mediaeval and earlier predecessors. Furthermore, because of its compact plan and modest size, Perth is one of the best-excavated mediaeval towns in Scotland. The results of these excavations are well documented,

## Marshall monument

The Museum was dedicated to the memory of a former Lord Provost of the city, Thomas Hay Marshall (of whom more in Chapter 11). His statue stands in the portico above which is the inscription, *TH Marshall Cives Grati* (The citizens thank TH Marshall). This refers to the fact that part of the cost of the statue was raised by public subscription. It is still referred to as the Marshall Monument.

The statue of Thomas Hay Marshall in the portico of the Museum and Art Gallery.

and many of the most interesting objects are on view in this building.

Although now a single building, Perth Museum and Art Gallery was built in two stages, separated by a century, and relating to two different learned societies. The eastern part, with its dome and huge portico of white pillars, was completed in 1824. It is based on the Pantheon in Rome and was clearly designed to complement the smaller building next door. It was designed by David Morison, the secretary of the Literary and Antiquarian Society of Perth, to exhibit the Society's collections and house its library, and is probably the oldest museum building in the United Kingdom still used for its original purpose. The Society, founded in 1784, was very much a part of the Scottish Enlightenment, which though centred in Edinburgh, flowered also in Perth.

The other society involved was the Perthshire Society of Natural Science, which was founded in 1867 and is still an important body in Perth today, holding regular meetings and producing important publications. It quickly built up a large collection of exhibits, which were housed in the purpose-built museum at 66 Tay Street, opened in 1883.

By the late 1920s, however, both the Natural Science and the Antiquarian collections had outgrown their museums, and the ability of the volunteer societies to manage them. They were taken over by Perth Council, which commissioned a large extension to the Marshall Monument so that both collections could be exhibited. This was opened by the

Duke and Duchess of York – later King George VI and Queen Elizabeth – on a very wet 10 August 1935. Following the opening ceremony, the Duke and Duchess were awarded the Freedom of Perth.

The new extension was built of honey coloured ashlar. It has an elegant porch, above which is an interesting coat of arms. There is a spacious entrance hall with a mosaic floor, a glazed dome and an impressive staircase leading to the dome of the original Marshall Monument, which is used for special art exhibitions. The extension comprises several large halls to display the museum's many collections, and stage important exhibitions. There is also a lecture theatre, and considerable basement storage. The combined building makes a fine full stop to the north end of George Street, and, along with the bow-fronted Georgian building next door, a pleasant vista for the visitor arriving from the Perth Bridge. John Gifford's description of the Museum and Art Gallery in the *Perth and Kinross* volume of 'The Buildings of Scotland' series as 'authoritarian civic architecture'[1] is amply justified.

Modern archaeological excavations, particularly prior to the building of the Marks & Spencer's store in the High Street (opened 1981) and the Concert Hall (opened 2005) have shed much light on burgh life in mediaeval Perth. Because of the anaerobic conditions in the dense, waterlogged silt washed down by the Tay, much organic material, such as leather, wood and even textiles, was well preserved, and so the excavations have yielded an enormous number of

Floodlit extension to the Museum and Art Gallery.

1930s Stalinesque representation of Perth's coat of arms.

1 *Perth and Kinross* by John Gifford. 'The Buildings of Scotland' series. Yale University Press, 2007. p. 605.

Glazed dome above the foyer in the museum extension.

important artefacts, many of which are now in the Perth Museum. The excavations in the High Street also revealed the foundations of several mediaeval buildings, including that of Perth's Parliament Hall, and Parliament Close, and below that the traces of earlier 12th century timber buildings.

A walrus ivory knife handle.
© Perth Museum & Art Gallery, Perth & Kinross Council.

*Above right:*
A mediaeval hammer.
© Perth Museum & Art Gallery, Perth & Kinross Council.

*Below:*
Concert Hall from the Air.

*Below right:*
Horsecross mosaic.

## Fine Art in Perth

Art lovers visiting Perth will not be disappointed. Perth & Kinross

In 2007 the collections in the Perth Museum were the first of any Scottish Local Authority to be designated 'A Recognised Collection of National Significance'.

Council cares for one of the oldest public collections in the UK, comprising over 1,000 paintings, including many old masters. It also has an impressive body of Scottish art, from the founding of the Scottish School to contemporary examples. Some of these are on permanent display: others are exhibited on special occasions, or in particular venues.

Two artists are particularly associated with Perth, although neither is a true 'son' of the city: Sir John Everett Millais (see Chapter 13) and John Duncan Fergusson (see Chapter 9).

## Perth Concert Hall

Perth's potential for music and the arts received a huge boost in 2005 when Her Majesty the Queen opened Perth Concert Hall. It was conceived as a millennium project in the late 1980s, and was the subject of a design competition in 1996. However, progress was slow and funding difficult to secure, but the people of Perth (especially Perth & Kinross Council) and the Gannochy Trust were not discouraged. Ultimately their faith was amply rewarded, and the effect on Perth's artistic endeavour and its economy has been enormous.

The building is located adjacent to the Museum and Art Gallery, just north of the line of the old city wall, in an area which in the 17th century was a horse market, and hence it is known as the 'Horse Cross'. This origin is illustrated by a mosaic on the pavement opposite the Concert Hall. The thoroughly modern glass and concrete structure, built on an oval footprint with a copper domed roof, has redefined the urban landscape of the area. Its flexible auditorium, small hall, and large foyer called the 'Threshold' can cater effectively for all manner of events from pop concerts for up to 1,800 people, to small gatherings of less than 100 guests sitting at tables. The

The modern glass and concrete Concert Hall.

foyer hosts exhibitions and receptions, and has a well-patronised café. It is readily accessible from, and gives easy access to, the commercial heart of the city.

In front of the Concert Hall is a four-sided clock tower, given to the people of Perth by the city's three Rotary Clubs.

### Perth Festival of the Arts

The peak event in Perth's cultural calendar is the Perth Festival of the Arts, which in 2011 celebrated its 40th anniversary. It takes place over ten days at the end of May in the Concert Hall and Theatre, and also in St John's Kirk and St Ninian's Cathedral. This festival regularly features the most famous orchestras from all over the world, classical and modern opera, theatre, jazz, folk music, and much else besides. In addition to the headline performances there is a festival fringe of exhibitions and local events.

Art for sale on Tay Street. A fringe event of the Perth Festival of the Arts.

The logo of the Perth Festival of the Arts. Courtesy Madeleine Hand.

The Fair Maid's House.
MAP 1 · N12

'Grace and Peace', the motto of the Glovers' Incorporation, above the door of the Fair Maid's House.

Perth has long had an impressive reputation as a centre for music and the arts. This is due to its cultural heritage extending back to the Stuart monarchs, and to its rich local arts scene, involving a huge number of committed local groups engaged in all kinds of music, theatre, art, literature, history and the sciences. That reputation has been immeasurably enhanced by the Concert Hall. In addition to entertainment of all types, the Concert Hall provides a versatile venue for conferences, and other large meetings that require its excellent 'breakout' and catering facilities.

Throughout the year, Perth Concert Hall has a very full programme of regular events, including the main Scottish orchestras, as well as pop, folk and trad concerts, award celebrations, brass band competitions, ice shows etc. It frequently attracts international artists from all over the world, and is regularly praised for its acoustics by the performers and audiences.

## Fair Maid's House and Lord John Murray's House

Behind the Concert Hall, on an ancient street called the North Port at its junction with Curfew Row and Blackfriars Wynd, is the Fair Maid's House, and next door to it, Lord John Murray's House. The Fair Maid's House is the oldest secular building in Perth, with elements dating from 1475, including a mediaeval wall (now exposed), which was part of the neighbouring Blackfriars Monastery, where King James I was murdered in 1437.

This is the building Scott described in his novel as the home of Simon Glover, the father of the Fair Maid Catharine and a senior member of the Glovers' Incorporation of Perth. The house was for 150 years the headquarters of the Glovers' Incorporation, and their motto, '*Grace and Peace*', is carved above the door. Tradition has it that the niche under the eaves of the south-western corner, overlooking Curfew Row, once housed Perth's curfew bell.

The property next door, known as Lord John Murray's House, was in fact the stables for his townhouse. Latterly it may have been converted into an arcaded shop, of a type that was quite common in Scotland at the time, although no others survive in Perth. The building was derelict for many years, but in the 1980s it was converted into a solicitor's office.

The niche in the corner of the Fair Maid's House and above it a carved face.

**The history of the ownership** of this building illustrates how the 1745 Uprising split many Perthshire families. Lord John Murray was the younger son of the First Duke of Atholl. He was MP for Perthshire 1734–1761, and at the same time a general in the Hanoverian army. He managed to stay out of trouble during the Uprising as his military service kept him in Europe at the critical time. His older brother, Lord George Murray, was also a notable general, but in the Jacobite army. Lord George died in exile after the failure at Culloden.

In 2010 the two properties were acquired by the Royal Scottish Geographical Society (RSGS), linked together and carefully restored and extended, winning a Scottish Civic Trust commendation.

Lord John Murray's House.

### Royal Scottish Geographical Society (RSGS)

The RSGS is a learned society with a worldwide membership of 2,500. Since its foundation in 1884 it has sought to advance the science of geography by sponsoring exploration, education and research. In this it works closely with the Scottish universities and other institutions. Its academic publication is *The Scottish Geographical Journal*, and it also produces a quarterly magazine, *The Geographer*, and numerous other books and pamphlets. One of its main activities is to sponsor a series of 50 illustrated talks by 'inspiring people' – explorers, ornithologists, geographers, and others – in several venues across Scotland.

The RSGS has relocated its headquarters and much of its extensive archive of

maps, books, photographs and artefacts from Glasgow to Perth. It has established its headquarters in Lord John Murray's House, and fitted out the Fair Maid's House as an education, information and exhibition centre. In doing so, it has added significantly to Perth's academic critical mass.

The objectives of the RSGS encapsulated in a picture of the globe and a wild flower meadow.
© RSGS

The logo of the Royal Scottish Geographical Society.
© RSGS

# Pullar Buildings

The Fair Maid's house looks out at the back of the Pullar Buildings, the front of which extends from the Concert Hall right up Mill Street and round onto Kinnoull Street. The two immensely long, 'relentlessly' regular, Renaissance façades provide a pleasing urban edge to Mill Street,

which contrasts starkly with the unsightly backs of the High Street shops on the south side of the street. The three-storey eastern block has recently been converted into a Premier Inn hotel and restaurant. Importantly, the façade has been retained. The western L-shaped block, which turns the corner from Mill Street onto Kinnoull Street, was converted into offices for Perth & Kinross Council in 2000, and is now called Pullar House. The four-storey extension along Kinnoull Street was redeveloped as housing. Old hydrant covers with the Perth coat of arms can still be seen.

On either side of the Kinnoull Street entrance to the Council offices are two large bronze plaques. On the left is a bas-relief portrait of Sir

**Sir Robert Pullar** was one of a group of hugely successful 19th century entrepreneurs in Perth. The coming of the railway enabled his small cleaning and dying business to expand across the whole of the UK. By the turn of the century it employed 2,600 people, had 300 branches and over 4,700 agencies. And yet in less than 20 years, it was practically all gone. The First World War, a changing industrial environment and undoubtedly poor management by the third generation of the Pullar family all contributed to the demise.

Robert Pullar, celebrating his 50th anniversary as a partner in the firm in 1898, and above it an illustration of the factory as it appeared in 1848. On the right is a matching plaque bearing the names of the employees of the firm who died in the two world wars.

## Multi-Storey Car Park

Behind the Council offices in Pullar House is a large new multi-storey car park which serves all the leisure and office facilities in the area. It is accessed from Kinnoull Street through a pend in the Pullar buildings.

## Perth Theatre

Opposite the western block of the Pullar buildings is the back of the Perth Theatre, and the narrow Cutlog Vennel, which leads to the theatre's front door on the High Street.

Drama has a very long history in Perth, with records of performances, in many different venues going back to the early 16th century. Perth's current building, an A-listed late Victorian theatre, was opened in 1901 and is one of Scotland's oldest theatres. It is also a very busy one, with a year-round programme of classical and popular drama, new writing, unique Perth productions, and touring shows – all with a leavening of music, comedy and dance. Its bijou 460-seat auditorium is typical of its period, decorated with gold leaf and plush red velvet, with rococo embellishments. It was the home of Scotland's first repertory company, and is a mainstay of Scotland's arts calendar.

At the time of writing, a £13m refurbishment of the theatre has commenced and is due to be completed in 2015. This will 'turn the theatre round' so that the main entrance will be off Mill Street, not far from the Concert Hall, and the new hotel in the eastern Pullar building. The plan will not alter the size or position of the main auditorium, nor the listed entrance from the High Street.

The other elements of the existing theatre, in particular the Studio theatre and the Red Rooms café-bar and restaurant, will be modernised and the complex incorporated into Mill Street's cultural quarter.

**Perth Theatre and Concert Hall** are both owned by Perth & Kinross Council, but managed by a single 'arms length' organisation called 'Horsecross'. This successful arrangement ensures that the programmes complement, rather than compete with each other. In 2011 425,000 people, from all over the UK, and abroad, attended events at these venues.

The late Victorian stage of Perth Theatre stage, decorated with gold leaf, plush velvet and roccoco embellishments. © Horsecross Perth.

Bordeaux House, now the Bothy restaurant. The original name Matthew Gloag & Son can be seen behind the new sign.
MAP 1 · L10

The 'swag' in the gable of the Bothy recalls that the origin of business was a wine Merchant's shop.

*Below:*
Sandeman bar-restaurant. Its original purpose as a public library is still very obvious.

## The Bothy, the Sandeman, and the Karnival Club

At the corners of Mill Street and Kinnoull Street are two buildings of considerable historical and aesthetic importance to Perth, which now contribute to the cultural and nightlife of the City. Bordeaux House, now The Bothy restaurant with its Famous Grouse Bar, was built in 1906 on the Kinnoull Street/ Mill Street corner, in Edwardian Renaissance style. It was the elegant headquarters of the wine and spirit firm, Matthew Gloag & Son,

**Professor Sandeman** was the heir to the Sandeman Port fortune. Sandeman's of Oporto had been founded a century earlier in 1790 by George Sandeman of Perth to import wine from Portugal. However, the wine which was fairly weak did not travel well on the long sea voyage to Britain, and the Sandeman firm experimented by adding brandy to the wine to aid its travelling qualities and bring out the sweet taste. Sandeman Port had a ratio of one part brandy to five parts wine.

The Sandeman family, though a century earlier than Perth's whisky entrepreneurs, were equally innovative. The firm introduced the first trademark into the business – the black Don with his Spanish bonnet representing sherry, and the Portuguese cape representing port, and so were the first to establish brand recognition in the market.

Archibald Sandeman's gift of the library to the City was said to have benefitted the citizens of Perth, young and old, more than any other civic project of the time.

producers of the Famous Grouse whisky (Chapter 5). In 1996 the company moved to new premises at Kinfauns, on Perth's eastern outskirts, and the ground floor and basement became a pub-restaurant.

On the other side of Kinnoull Street corner is The Sandeman. Opened in 1898, it was built, like Bordeaux House, in the Renaissance style with red sandstone, and has an unusual pepper-pot clock tower on the corner (sadly no longer working). This was Perth's first public reference and lending library, and was a gift to the city from the estate of Professor Archibald Sandeman, who died in

1893. In 1994 the books were moved to the AK Bell building, and sometime later The Sandeman opened as a bar-restaurant.

Farther up Mill Street, next to the North Church is the former Sharp's Educational Institution, the main entrance of which is on North Methven Street. It is an interesting Italianate building, B-listed, with a central tower of four storeys and two deep three-storey wings. It is set back and fenced off from the streets in its former playground with some mature trees screening it from South Methven Street. It was built in 1860 with money from James Sharp, a wealthy Perth baker, and served its purpose as a school until 1942, when the pupils were moved to the Perth Academy building in Viewlands. Thereafter it was used as offices until 2002 when it became a bar-restaurant. It has recently undergone a major refurbishment and re-opened as a nightclub – the Karnival Club.

# North Church

Across Kinnoull Street, and still on Mill Street, is the imposing North Church, built in 1881. Designed like a basilica in the Italian Romanesque style, the heavy pillared porch is set up from the road, its round-headed arches leading the eye to the tall lancet windows above. It makes a very impressive structure. The North Church and its extensive halls and offices occupy most of the pend between Mill Street and the upper end of the High Street.

**Perth Street Pastors**

The North Church, with its extensive halls in the Centre for much of the Christian outreach in Perth. One of the important projects has been Perth Street Pastors – the first group of Street Pastors in Scotland. At weekends and public holidays, groups of four pastors, all members of Christian churches and thoroughly trained, walk the streets of Perth city centre from 10pm to 4am, making themselves available to speak to and help any who are sad, depressed or even suicidal. The presence of the pastors has significantly reduced crime and anti-social behaviour.

*Top:*
Sharp's Educational Institute. Now the Karnival Klub night spot.
MAP 1 · K10

*Left:*
The North Church.
MAP 1 · L10

*Right:*
The Sandeman 'pepper-pot' clock tower.

## The Playhouse

Facing the North Church across the bus stances which occupy this part of Mill Street is the Playhouse, a stylish Art Deco cinema built in 1933 in only nine weeks. The façade above the entrance and the adjacent shops is typical of the era, and consists of marble and red brick with wrap around Crittall windows. It still contains many of the original art deco fittings and furnishings. When it was built it could seat 1,700 patrons. In the 1970s it was divided into three cinemas, and then in 1999 it was refurbished and extended to seven screens, and most recently it has installed an IMAX screen. It shows a full range of Hollywood blockbusters and other films.

## West Mill Street

Mill Street ends at North Methven street, but the line of the street continues as West Mill Street, leading to the City Mills and Hal o' the Wynd's house.

# CHAPTER ELEVEN

# Perth's Georgian New Town

FOLLOWING THE opening of the Perth Bridge in 1771, Perth experienced a period of rapid expansion, doubling its population to 15,000 in 30 years. This was managed by an enterprising group of wealthy business families, who were in charge of all the levers of power in Perth from the 1790s until 1832. George Penny in *Traditions of Perth* (1836) refers to them as 'The Beautiful Order, an abominable system calculated for the complete subversion of the liberties of the citizens'. Two of them were particularly prominent at the turn of the century: Thomas Anderson and his son-in-law, Thomas Hay Marshall. To promote their ambitious plans, they employed the young Robert Reid, a friend of Thomas Hay Marshall and a rising star among architects, who became a celebrity and later the King's architect on account of his plans for Edinburgh's New Town. Together they developed the streets overlooking the Inches, in particular Charlotte Street, Atholl Street, Atholl Place, Atholl Crescent and Rose Terrace in the north, and Marshall Place, overlooking the South Inch. These and the adjacent side streets make up Perth's Georgian New Town. They are still the most elegant streets in Perth.

**Thomas Hay Marshall**

Marshall's meteoric rise to prominence was built on solid family foundations, which in turn were grounded in 'The Beautiful Order'. His father had been a founder member of the Perth Banking Company, City Treasurer and was elected Lord Provost in 1784. Thomas was born in 1770, entered the Council in 1790, was City Treasurer at 21 and Bailie at 22. By this time he was involved in property development with his future father-in-law Thomas Anderson, who was a wealthy linen manufacturer, and a leading burgess in Perth.

He was elected Lord Provost in 1800, and served another term from 1804. He died in 1808, at the age of only 38. His funeral, attended by the Duke of Atholl, was the biggest Perth had ever seen and the obituaries were fulsome. Furthermore, his reputation survived to such an extent that 16 years after his death, public subscriptions contributed to the cost of his statue, which stands in the portico of the Perth Museum and Art Gallery – the Marshall Monument. Sculpted by a local stonemason named Cochrane, it is the only statue in Perth of a famous Perth citizen.

Thomas Hay Marshall.

## The Northern Georgian New Town

### Blackfriars

The large wedge of land between the City wall (Mill Street) and the North Inch was given to the Dominican Order by King Alexander II in 1234

Blackfriars lives on in this street name.

to establish a monastery. In due course the Blackfriars Monastery became the most important of Perth's religious houses, with royal apartments used by the Scottish kings for 200 years, and appropriate chambers which regularly hosted meetings of the Scottish Parliament. It was also in Blackfriars Monastery that King James I was assassinated in 1437.

Blackfriars latterly became the site of the mediaeval North Port suburb, an out-of-town area with a concentration of unsavoury industries such as tanning. By the late 18th century it had become densely built-up and was ripe for redevelopment. It was Thomas Anderson who realised the potential of the area and negotiated the acquisition of the land, and it was Marshall who built (literally) on his father-in-law's foundations.

## Charlotte Street

The visitor who wishes to explore Perth's Georgian New Town should start from the landfall of the Perth Bridge and walk along Charlotte Street to the North Inch. The houses in the smart terrace on the right-hand

### King James I and Tennis

Modern lawn tennis is derived from a game that is now called 'Royal' or 'Real' tennis, which was first played by monks in France in the 12th century. It was the 'Sport of Kings' long before horse racing claimed that title. Henry V, who reigned from 1413–1422, was the first English monarch known to have played the game, but in Scotland it was well established before that. James I was an enthusiast and contemporary records note that the Blackfriars monastery 'provides a fair playing place for tennis'. This would have had a paved surface and be walled all round, like the court in Falkland Palace in Fife, which was built in 1539 and is the oldest 'royal' tennis court in the world.

Tennis, however, was to be James's undoing. Tennis balls kept rolling down the flood drains, beneath the monastery, and into the Lade. And so the king ordered the outfall of the drain to be bricked up. Later that same month, on February 20 1437, assassins broke into the King's apartments. In desperation he wrenched up the floorboards of the room, and dropped into the drain – from which, however, there was now no escape, and he was brutally hacked down. His wife, Joan Beaufort, however, escaped with her infant son, now James II, and assumed the Regency of Scotland.

For Perth, then the capital of Scotland, this was to have even more serious consequences than the death of the King. The Royal Family felt insecure in Perth and moved the royal household and court to Edinburgh – which in due course became the capital of Scotland. So tennis casts a very long shadow across Perth.

gardens and iron railings, and Atholl Crescent's ambiance in particular has been seriously damaged by car parking. No. 1 Atholl Crescent is the discrete home of the Royal Perth Golfing Society. With its hushed ambience, wood-panelled walls, deep leather chairs, billiard rooms and male only membership, it is a bastion of Old Perth Society.

side were the first of the planned New Town, and were built in the 1790s. They are now somewhat obscured by the approach road to the bridge. A badge above the front door of No. 1 advertises the fact that the building was insured against fire. On the left, at the end of the terrace, turning the corner into the North Port, is the A-listed Charlotte House, the bow windows of which look up Charlotte Street and across the North Inch. This building, with its Doric columns supporting the first floor balcony and iron balustrade, is one of the finest in Perth.

Opposite Charlotte House is a large statue of Prince Albert by William Brodie, erected in 1864. He is dressed in the robes of a Knight of the Thistle.

## Atholl Place and Atholl Crescent

The west side of Charlotte Street, opposite the North Inch, consists of two terraces, Atholl Place, and Atholl Crescent (A-listed), which are set back from the road, and enjoy open views across the North Inch. Unfortunately, they are now bereft of their original landscaped front

Provost's lamp outside No. 4 Atholl Crescent.

*Above right:*
Masonic Temple from the altar looking towards Peddie's King Alexander I mural.

Mural showing King Alexander I of Scotland reviewing the work of the building of Scone Abbey in 1115.

**Masonic Lodge** The continuous roofline of Atholl Crescent is interrupted at No. 5, the central building of the Crescent, which stands forward from the rest, with a gable and rose window to the front. In 1932 the building was acquired and redeveloped for 'Lodge Scoon and Perth No. 3' to become one of the largest and finest Masonic Temples in Scotland. The London artist and mason, Thomas Hutchison Peddie, who had Perth connections, decorated the walls of the temple with four large murals (18ft in height) and several smaller ones. The most interesting of these on the north wall depicts King Alexander I of Scotland reviewing the work of the building of Scone Abbey in 1115.

Lodge Scoon and Perth No. 3 is one of the oldest, if not the oldest, lodge in Scotland. Its earliest extant document, 'The Mutual Agreement' is dated 1658, and refers to the foundation of the Lodge by the masons constructing the great Abbey of Scone, 'four hundredth thriescore and five yeires or thereby' previously. Without taking account of the 'thereby', this gives a foundation date of 1193. However, the Abbey was actually founded by King Alexander I in 1114 and it may well have been that the Lodge was established then, or soon after, as Peddie's mural suggests.

Mural showing James VI at the ceremony when he was entered as a Fellow of the Craft of the Lodge.

The Mutual Agreement also mentions that King James VI 'by his own desire was entered frieman, measone, and Fellow of Craft of the Lodge'. Peddie's mural on the east wall of the temple depicts this event, which took place on the 15 April 1601.

In the lodge refectory there is a stained-glass panel illustrating the crowning of King Robert the Bruce at Scone in 1306. This was a special exhibit made for the 1901 Glasgow International Exhibition. The artist was David Gauld (1865–1936), one of the 'Glasgow Boys'. Contemporary records indicate that originally there

*The Fair Maid of Perth and the Carthusian Monk*, by TH Peddie.
© Perth Museum & Art Gallery, Perth & Kinross Council.

**The Fair Maid of Perth and a Carthusian Monk**

Peddie painted a number of Scottish historical characters, including Mary Queen of Scots, Bonny Prince Charlie and *The Fair Maid of Perth and a Carthusian Monk*. This last picture illustrates an incident in Scott's novel, when the Fair Maid meets a Carthusian monk on Kinnoull Hill for religious devotions. The view of the Tay meandering through the Carse of Gowrie is instantly recognisable today. The picture is in the Perth Museum and Art Gallery.

The crowning of King Robert the Bruce in Scone, 1306. Stained-glass panel by David Gault.

Plaster design on the dome above the spiral stair.

Moulding showing rose and thistle, but no shamrock of Ireland.

were five panels. Four of these were given to the Lodge in 1930; one is still missing. Any information about the missing panel would be welcomed by the Lodge.

Like several of the other buildings in the Crescent, the Lodge has a circular staircase with a domed decorated plaster ceiling and a cupola. There is also an original Adam style fireplace. Interestingly, one of the mouldings on the fireplace shows a thistle and a rose intertwined, but not a shamrock. This probably dates the building to before 1801, when Ireland was incorporated into the United Kingdom.

The Lodge is open for visitors on Doors Open Days.

## Rose Terrace

Opposite Atholl Crescent, forming part of the western boundary for the North Inch, is Rose Terrace, the jewel in the crown of Perth's northern new town. The corner block with Atholl Street is a magnificent pavilion. Now converted into flats, it was originally intended to be Thomas Hay Marshall's personal mansion. Sadly,

### Bruce Panel

The panel records the second crowning of King Robert the Bruce. Following the murder of Red Comyn in Dumfries, Bruce headed to Scone, where he was crowned without delay by Bishop Lamberton of St Andrews on 27 March 1306. However, the next day, Isabella, the Countess of Buchan, arrived in Scone. As the sister of the Earl of Fife, she claimed the hereditary right to place the King of Scots on the Stone of Destiny for the coronation. Isabella was not a lady to be ignored and so on 29 March the ceremony was repeated.

The circlet of gold that the Countess holds still forms the foundation of the Scottish crown. This crown, although refashioned and greatly embellished for James V is by far the oldest crown in the UK. Isabella was to pay dearly for her loyalty. Following Bruce's defeat a few weeks later in the Battle of Methven, she was captured, and imprisoned for four years in a cage in the tower of the Castle of Berwick upon Tweed.

Detail from the stained-glass panel showing Isabella, Countess of Buchan, with the circlet of gold, which still forms the foundation of the Scottish crown.

however, the matching pavilion at the northern end of the terrace was never built, robbing the street of its designed symmetry.

**Old Academy Building** The centre block of Rose Terrace, completed in 1807, is the masterpiece. Built on three plots donated by Marshall, it was designed by Robert Reid. It brought together, into a single prestigious building, several schools in Perth, including the Grammar School and the Academy. Called at the time, 'Perth Seminaries', it is now referred to as the 'Old Academy', and is A-listed. There are a number of remarkable internal features, including two oval staircases, and an Adamesque octagonal classroom with an elaborately plastered domed ceiling. The statue of Britannia with the clock and lion were added in 1886. In 1932 a new Academy was built in the western suburbs, and since then the building has languished.

In front of the Old Academy

building is a modern sculpture, *Season, Time and Place*, by Frances Pelly (1991), consisting of an octagonal arrangement of stone slabs. The inscription on the inner stones reads: 'My garden side by side native plants together.'

Rose Terrace overlooking the North Inch.

Thomas Hay Marshall's pavilion on the corner of Rose Terrace.
MAP 1 · M13

The Old Academy building.
MAP 1 · L14

Oval staircase in the Old Academy building.

Britannia and the clock above the Old Academy building.

The octagonal classroom protrudes from the back of the Old Academy building.

Sculpture – *Season, Time and Place* by Frances Pelly.

*Opposite page, top left:*
Perth's Theatre Royal, now the restaurant Deans @ Let's Eat.
MAP 1 · L13

Georgian House on corner of Barossa Place and Melville Street.
MAP 1 · J14

## Atholl Street and Adjacent Streets

Atholl Street and the streets behind Rose Terrace, including Barossa Place, named after Lord Lynedoch's famous victory, are also part of Perth's Georgian New Town.

### Rose Anderson

Rose Terrace was named after Rose, the daughter of Thomas Anderson and wife of Thomas Hay Marshall. The marriage, bringing together two very important Perth families, promised much. Rose, however, soon became the talk of the town for other reasons, which set the lace curtains of Georgian Perth twitching.

After their marriage, she lived with Thomas in an apartment in one of the new buildings in Charlotte Street, while the splendid pavilion in Rose Terrace was being built. Across the street, Lord Elgin (he of the Elgin Marbles) had lodgings. When Thomas was in London or Edinburgh on business, Rose and Elgin were seen to exchange signals and send each other messages. There were assignations on Kinnoull Hill, late night visits to Rose's apartment by Lord Elgin, and they even walked arm in arm on the streets of Perth.

A contemporary, disreputable ditty, 'Rose Anderson', a version of which has been recorded by Jean Redpath, describes a confrontation between Lord Elgin and Marshall. This may or may not have taken place, but whatever happened, Elgin left Perth. Rose then took up with a military man, Dr Harrison, to whom she sent love letters and gifts. In 1796, in the face of the scandal, Rose left Perth, first for Edinburgh and then Yorkshire, where she again met Lord Elgin. She returned to Edinburgh in 1800, where she stayed with her parents, but continued to consort with officers of the Royal Artillery.

Neither Rose nor her husband ever lived in the beautiful pavilion in Rose Terrace.

Although less salubrious than those streets facing the North Inch, they include many B-listed buildings. Among them, on the corner of Atholl Street and Kinnoull Street is Jamieson's Buildings, constructed in 1820 as Perth's Theatre Royal. This theatre saw the first dramatisation of *The Fair Maid of Perth* in 1828, only a few months after the novel's publication. The ground floor is now occupied by one of Perth's best restaurants, Deans @ Let's Eat.

## St Ninian's Episcopalian Cathedral

St Ninian's Cathedral, at the corner of Atholl Street and North Methven Street, was consecrated in 1850, so is Victorian rather than Georgian. However, it contributes greatly to the built environment of the area. It was the first Episcopalian cathedral to be built in Britain after the Reformation, and serves the diocese of St Andrews, Dunkeld and Dunblane. Its foundation was promoted by two aristocratic laymen, the 18th Lord Forbes and Walter Boyle, later the Sixth Earl of Glasgow, to be the visible evidence of the resurgence of the Episcopalian tradition in Scotland, and to provide appropriate

accommodation for a bishop and a team of clergy. Their ambitious plans, which included a bell tower and spire of imposing proportions that 'would be a commanding feature in any distant view of the Fair City' (William Butterfield, the original architect), did not materialise because of problems with the foundations, and probably the cost. There is, however, a gilded fleche. A number of different architects were involved with design changes and alterations, which continued until 1936.

Nevertheless, the final result is very pleasing. The nave and choir are of impressive dimensions, white painted and divided from the aisles by stone arches. A high rood screen separating the nave from the choir carries gold painted wooden statues of the Crucifix, Mary the Mother of Christ, and St John the Divine. Beneath the statues is the inscription: *Deus delixit mundum ut suum unigenitum daret* (which may be

The west façade of St Ninian's Cathedral with flower beds.

The fleche of St Ninian's Cathedral.
MAP 1 · J13

The high Rood Screen in St Ninian's Cathedral.

Bishop's throne, St Ninian's.

St Ninian's, Kinnoull window.

freely translated as, 'God so loved the world that He gave his only begotten Son'). Within the choir are carved oak stalls for the clergy and choir, and nearer the high altar the Bishop's throne, with a richly carved oak canopy. The high altar itself incorporates a slab of Iona Marble from the original altar of 1850. The nave has an impressive collection of stained glass by Burlison and Grylls. One of these, the Kinnoull window on the south wall, depicts the Raising of Lazarus. The Earl of Kinnoull is depicted as Lazarus, and members of his family as the bystanders.

The Victorian pews have been removed and replaced by more comfortable and flexible seating, which contributes to the church's attraction as a venue for concerts and other events.

The church has a very strong musical tradition, and hosts a number of music scholarships. The organ, by Miller of Dundee, has been completely refurbished, and is said to be one of the finest in Scotland.

## The Southern part of Perth's Georgian New Town

The southern element of Perth's Georgian New Town consists of the single-sided street overlooking the South Inch, referred to generally as Marshall Place, and a few houses in each of the adjacent streets. The street begins at the Fergusson Gallery at the corner of Tay Street, and stretches westwards to the railway bridge at the station. At the junction with Scott Street, Marshall Place becomes King James Place, and from the junction of King Street it is called Kings Place. For the purposes of this book it will all be called Marshall Place.

## Marshall Place

Next to the Fergusson Gallery are offices (Belhaven House), which occupy a plot that formerly contained a pump-house for the waterworks. Then there is The Archery, a block of contemporary flats built in 1994.

The Georgian section of Marshall Place begins at its junction with the Edinburgh Road and Princes Street. The outline plan was drawn up by Robert Reid in 1805, and Reid himself designed the first two terraces, Nos 1–14 and 15–28, which lie between the traffic lights at the Edinburgh Road and the church of St Leonard's-in-the-Fields. These are the buildings that catch the eye of visitors approaching Perth from Edinburgh. They were completed in 1830, and are the pinnacle of Reid's achievements in Perth.

Each symmetrical terrace consists of a massive corner house, and a matching centrepiece of two houses, joined together by two terraces of five houses each. The corner and central blocks consist of a half-basement and three storeys, while the intermediate houses have the basement, two storeys and an attic. A forestair leads from the front door down to the garden, which is bounded by a low stone wall on which were railings, with a wrought iron arch to hold a lamp over the front gate.

Sadly, most of the railings and many of the arches have gone and been replaced by hedges. Several of the houses have had their stonework painted and astragals have been lost from some of the windows and fan lights. Notwithstanding these

*Marshall Place from the South Inch, in spring before the leaves obscure the view.*

*Left:*
No. 14 Marshall Place, designed by Robert Reid of Edinburgh New Town fame.

Nos 7 and 8 Marshall Place. The centre block of the first Robert Reid terrace.

*Clockwise:*
The tower and crown spire of
St Leonard's-in-the-Fields
across the South Inch.
MAP 1 · L3

Crown spire of St Leonard's
rising above a signal gantry on
the railway viaduct.

Part of Reid's middle terrace
with St Leonard's-in-the-
Fields at the end.

changes, which give a patchwork
appearance to what should be a
unified exterior, these two terraces
remain an excellent example of
Georgian domestic architecture.

Reid intended there to be five
terraces, two to the east of 14 houses
each, and then three shorter terraces
to the west, matching those he had
already built, but without the
centrepiece houses. However,

building was delayed, and the plots
for the first of the three short terraces
were sold to build what is now the St
Leonard's-in-the-Fields Church. The
middle terrace, however, was built to
designs based on Reid's plans but
modified by William Mackenzie, the
city architect. It consists of two
massive corner blocks and three
smaller houses between.
Unfortunately the corner blocks do
not quite match Reid's corner blocks,
nor indeed each other, but the
differences are not immediately
apparent to the untrained eye, and
the overall effect is very pleasing.

Only the first corner block of the
third terrace was built, the rest of the
street to the west being given over to
Victorian detached and semi-
detached villas. One of them is the
headquarters of the Aberdeen Angus
Cattle Society.

In 1849 the first (wooden) railway bridge was opened, carrying the line between Perth and Dundee. From the bridge the track is carried on a viaduct over Tay Street and then behind the church and houses in Marshall Place, cutting off part of their gardens. While this resulted in a considerable loss of amenity, it was better than the alternative, which was to build the railway station on the South Inch.

## Statue of Sir Walter Scott

Standing on the edge of the South Inch and facing down King Street is a lifesize statue of a toga-clad Sir Walter Scott and his deerhound, Maida.

## St Leonard's-in-the-Fields

This pretty church with its buttresses, clerestory windows and its four-arched crown spire faces out from Marshall Place across the South Inch.

This unusual spire, which can be seen through the trees of the park by travellers approaching Perth along the Edinburgh Road, is an important landmark. Built in Scots Gothic Revival style by architect John J Stevenson, a relation of the Stevenson lighthouse builders, it was opened in 1885. The crown spire is modelled on that of St Giles' in Edinburgh, but with four arches rather than eight. The octagonal apse derives from the Church of the Holy Rood in Stirling. However, in contrast to the elaborate exterior, the inside is quite plain.

## St Leonard's Bank

The transition between Georgian and Victorian architecture continues along St Leonard's Bank, which lies at right angles to Marshall Place, overlooking the north-west corner of the South Inch. This was the site of the St Leonard's Priory, the remains of which are buried under the adjacent railway embankment. The Parklands Hotel occupies the first two buildings of this terrace. The hotel and the related restaurant at 63 Tay Street are highly rated, and committed to the Cittaslow movement in Perth (see Chapter 19).

**Church Unions**

The congregation resulted from a union of St Leonard's and Trinity churches in 1982. More recently, it has been united with the High Kirk of St John, and one Minister is now in charge of both parishes and church buildings.

Statue of Sir Walter Scott with his deerhound, Maida.
MAP 1 · K3

Parklands Hotel on St Leonard's Bank, overlooking the snowdrops on the South Inch.
MAP 1 · I13

CHAPTER TWELVE

# 'Twixt City Wall and Railway

THERE HAVE BEEN settlements outwith Perth's city wall since the 12th century, mostly in the west, clustered around the City Mills, and in the north around the Blackfriars Monastery. In times of war or siege, when the gates of the city were closed, the inhabitants of these houses presumably retreated to safety behind the city wall.

The mediaeval defences were still functional at the time of the 1745 Uprising, but thereafter a period of peace coincided with a rapid increase in population, and the city burst through its mediaeval constrictions in many places, especially to the west of the city wall, extending the lines of the High Street and South Street. There was space in this new part of Perth for housing, commercial and civic buildings. Then, in 1845, the railway came to Perth, creating a western boundary which defined a distinct area of Perth, between the city wall and the railway line. This sector has much to interest the visitor.

## The Old High Street

Perth High Street pierced the city wall at the Turret Port, a fortified gate and bridge over the Lade, at the site of the present crossroads with Methven Street. From the Turret Port the High Street continued into the congested area associated with the City Mills. Here it is known,

paradoxically, as the 'Old' High Street, although it cannot be older than the main part of the street.

## St Paul's Church

In the 1790s, North and South Methven Streets were built along the line of the western city wall, on top

The spire of St Paul's Church, focal point of the High Street. MAP1·J9

As well as the clock, the tower of St Paul's contains a bell with the inscription 'Thomas Mears, London'. George Penny in Traditions of Perth writes that one of the bells from St John's was removed to St Paul's. This may be Perth's 'Common Bell', referred to in the city records of 1652, and in use in St John's from the early 17th century until 1804. It called the citizens to work on weekdays at 4am and 6am, and on Sundays for services at 9am, 11am, 2pm and 6pm. It was first cast in 1520, probably by George Wagheven of Mechlin, but was sent to Thomas Mears in London in 1805 to be recast, perhaps because it had cracked. A 'rubbing' preserved in Perth Museum records an inscription on the original bell:

*Johannes Baptista vocor*
*Nos autem gloriare opportet in cruce*
*Domini nostri Jhesu Christie*
*Anno domini 1520*
*Tacto vox clamantios in deserto – Parate*
*Viam*

(John the Baptist I am called
We must glory in the cross
of our Lord Jesus Christ
Anno Domini 1520
I am the voice crying in the wilderness
– Prepare the Way).

The bell in St Paul's, probably from St John's Kirk. Courtesy of the Perth & Kinross Heritage Trust.

of the Lade (which had been culverted). One of the early buildings in this area was St Paul's Church, which was built to relieve the pressure of Perth's expanding population on St John's. Opened in 1807, it stands on the corner of the Old High Street and South Methven Street, and is set within its own square, St Paul's Square. It is a large, octagonal building in a castellated gothic style with pepper pot turrets and a 60 foot dome rising to a glass cupola. Because of the slight bend in the High Street, St Paul's with its clock tower and spire forms an effective focal point for the view up the street from the centre of the city, and is therefore a very important element of Perth's urban landscape.

Internally, the church was in the austere style of the Presbyterian 'preaching station' of the time, with a capacity for a congregation of 1,200 ranged in pews and galleries focused on the pulpit from which the minister delivered his sermons. The building was closed in 1986 and has become derelict. At the time of writing it is sheathed in scaffolding, and there are plans to convert it into an Indian restaurant.

## The City Mills and Granary

The Mills were situated outside the city wall (see David Simon's map in Chapter 2), just north-west of the Old High Street. The Mills were well established on this site before the 12th century, when King David I granted ten shillings from his income from the Mills to Scone Abbey. In

into a hotel in 1971. It comprised an undershot mill wheel and two flour (wheat) mills, as well as the adjacent granary, which has been converted into offices and apartments by the National Trust for Scotland.

The Lade approaches the mill through the hotel garden, where it makes a fine backdrop for wedding photographs etc. It then shoots underneath the hotel foyer and public bar, where parts of the water wheel are preserved, and the water can be seen through viewing panels in the floor. It is well worth buying a drink in the bar, just to see it!

The other notable architectural feature in this hotel is the ballroom with its gallery and magnificent king-post roof.

From the Upper Mills the water passes under the bridge on West Mill Street to the Lower City Mills, where

1374, King Robert II gave the Mills to the town. By the 19th century there were two pairs of mills in the complex.

Perth's City Mills, in particular the Lower City Mills, are a unique survival from the late 18th century. At that time practically every town in Scotland with a large rural hinterland would have had similar mills. Now only Perth's mills remain.

From West Mill Street a cobbled courtyard opens up, in the top corner of which is the front door of the Mercure Hotel, known to everyone in Perth as the City Mills Hotel. This is the A-listed Upper City Mills, built in the late 1770s and converted

Mercure Hotel, King-pin roof
over ballroom.

oats and barley were milled until the Second World War. This mill has been restored, and received a UK Civic Trust Award as a working mill visitor attraction. However, the mill works are disused, and closed to visitors, except on Doors Open Day. Nevertheless, the machinery, including the huge mill wheel 15ft wide (and with a diameter of 15ft), is all in place, and capable of being restored to working condition.

## Hal o' the Wynd's House

Just opposite the Lower Mills, on the ancient lane called 'Mill Wynd', is Hal o' the Wynd's House – (see 'The Fair Maid's Trail, Chapter 16).

# Carthusian Monastery

In 1429 King James I established the Carthusian or Charterhouse Monastery on a site just outside the western city wall by the South Street Port. James's purpose may have been to encourage the renewal of religious life in Scotland, but it was also to provide a site for a new Royal Mausoleum. This is as good an indication as any that Perth was in fact the capital of Scotland at the time. The monastery prospered and James was buried there following his murder in 1437. Also buried there were his Queen, Joan Beaufort, in 1445, and more than a century later in 1541, Queen Margaret Tudor, widow of James IV who was killed at Flodden, and sister of King Henry VIII of England.

## The Charterhouse Memorial Monument

In the monastery grounds on the corner of Hospital Street and King Street provides a record of these burials. The monument is surmounted by a crown above the royal monogram, JR I (James Rex First), and the date 1437. The small garden at the foot of the monument is tended by the Perth Soroptimists.

## King James VI Hospital

The A-listed King James VI Hospital stands on the site of the Carthusian Monastery. It was Perth's third hospital since the Reformation in 1559. In the anarchy following that event, the mediaeval hospitals run by religious orders that cared for the sick and orphaned were closed down, with dire consequences, no doubt, for those in need. Ten years later, in 1569, the first post-Reformation hospital was founded by Royal Charter in the name of King James VI.

Possible royal grave slab mounted in St John's Kirk.

## A Royal Grave-Slab?

The monastery was completely destroyed during the Reformation, and nothing now remains above the ground. However, there is a large weathered grave-slab of Tournai marble, wide enough to cover two tombs, mounted vertically at the east end of St John's Kirk, adjacent to the Great East Window and largely obscured by a glass wall. The slab would have had two brass effigies fixed to it, but these have been lost. However the outline and fixing points remain. Experts believe the slab was made for an aristocrat, but are sceptical about claims it was for James I and his queen, Joan Beaufort, believing that it is more likely that it was for one of the Earls of Gowrie. However, tradition has it that the monks of the monastery, or perhaps some of Perth's citizens, rescued the slab during the turmoil of the Reformation, and later it was erected in the Kirk.

A renewed interest in the precise location of King James's remains has been kindled by the finding of the tomb of Richard III of England in Leicester.

James was only two years old in 1569, and the royal authority for the Charter was vested in the Regent, the Earl of Moray. Moray granted revenues for the hospital from the former monastic and religious properties in Perth, which had been forfeited to the Crown, and delegated the administration of the hospital to the Minister and Kirk Session of St John's. When King James came of age in 1587, he granted the hospital a second Royal Charter, confirming the details in the first. The site of this original Hospital, referred to in 1573

The south face of the King James VI Hospital.
MAP 1 · J7

as a 'tour for mony puir folkis to luge in', is not known.

In 1590 the second hospital was built at St Mary's Chapel, adjacent to the old Bridge of Perth. This continued to function until it was demolished by Cromwell's troops in 1651 to provide stone for the Citadel on the South Inch. For the next hundred years, Perth appears to have been without a hospital.

The hospital we see today was erected in 1750, nearly 200 years after the original charter. It is a very large building, four storeys high, with an attic, and built on an 'H' plan. It is one of Perth's most important mid 18th century buildings.

The original entrance to the hospital was on the south face, through a pillared and pedimented doorway, which is now a window. High above this door is a plaque with the date '1750'. The current entrance

is on the north front through a simpler doorway. Above that is another plaque, which bears the somewhat misleading inscription 'Founded by King James VI, 1587'. As we have seen, the original Charter was in 1569. It was confirmed in 1587 and this building constructed in 1750.

Above the central 'H' is an octagonal belfry covered with an ogee dome and copper weathercock. This and the bell within it were salvaged from the magnificent House of Nairne near Bankfoot, north of Perth, which was the home of the Second Lord Nairne, a prominent Jacobite. The house was forfeited following the Uprising in 1745, and demolished in 1764.

From the start, the hospital was intended to be a poor-house, a school, an infirmary and a reformatory for vagrants. However, by 1813 financial pressures and social changes caused the managers to allow the poor to live outwith the hospital and receive financial support. Then, in 1836, the Perth City and County Infirmary opened and took over most of the care of the sick and infirm. Thereafter, although the charitable work continued, most of the building was let for housing.

In 1975 financial support from the Gannochy Trust enabled the building to be completely refurbished, creating 21 well appointed flats, which are let at rates below the market rent. Throughout all the changes, the Trustees' Room with its wood panels (on which are recorded the names of the original donors to the hospital), has been preserved.

The hospital is now overseen by the Ministers and Elders of St John's Kirk and Letham St Mark's Kirk. Its upkeep is maintained by the rent from the flats and income from farmland bequeathed to the hospital in the 17th and 18th centuries.

*Top:*
Date stone on the south face of the Hospital – '1750'.

Plaque on the north face of the Hospital – 'Founded by King James the Sixth 1587'.

Belfry on the King James VI Hospital.

King James VI Hospital, Trustees' Room.

the Choragic Monument of Lysicrates which dates from 334BC and was built to commemorate success in a dance festival, and to honour the choreographer Lysicrates. The monument in Athens was much admired and copied in the 1800s. The example above the entrance to St Leonard's Church is a faithful representation (unlike the Burns monument on Calton Hill in Edinburgh). Since 1982 the building has been used as an auction house.

## Former St Leonard's Church

Close to the King James VI Hospital and facing down Canal Street, which it closes off in style, is the B-listed former St Leonard's Parish Church. It was designed by the City architect WFM Mackenzie, and completed in 1836. Mackenzie, like his contemporaries David Morison (Perth Museum & Art Gallery) and Adam Anderson (Fergusson Gallery), looked back to classical times for inspiration. He found it in Athens, in

## Perth Railway Station

At the height of the railway mania in Scotland, four competing companies each applied to build a station on the South Inch, and a public enquiry was required to get them to agree to a single location. Eventually a site was chosen at the south-west corner of the city centre, and the new station was designed and built between 1847 and 1849, with the Station Hotel following later. The architects were

Perth Railway Station from the south. The line on which the train is standing, the adjacent platforms, the low roof covering them and the octagonal tower behind are all parts of the original station.
MAP 1 · G3

Sir William Tite, a prominent railway architect from London, and A&A Heiton of Perth.

The station's splendid Tudor Gothic façade, with its octagonal tower topped by a slated spire, opened straight onto a large open square, with the north–south railway tracks running behind the station buildings, and the Dundee line curving away to the east. There was a huge porch on the front of the building to shelter travellers arriving and departing from the station.

In its Victorian heyday, Perth Railway station was the centre of a veritable spider's web of connections to every part of Scotland. Queen Victoria's fascination with Scotland had captured the imagination of London Society, and tourism was booming. George Earl captured the mood in 1895 with two pictures

showing the hunting/shooting/fishing fraternity on holiday. *Going North* featured King's Cross Station, and *Coming South* Perth Station.

In 1885, to cope with the increased traffic, the porch was demolished and a new double line built in front of the station. The

The original Victorian railway station which is still intact behind the modern façade.
© Perth & Kinross Council.

*Coming South* by George Earl. Perth Station in 1895.
© of the National Railway Museum, Science and Society Picture Library.

massive arched wall that was required to support the roof over this new line obscured the view of the original station from the square in front. Then in 1992 a new modern entrance hall and booking office completed the desecration of the station's former splendour.

Nevertheless, the Victorian structure is still intact, including the original clock and Queen Victoria's waiting room. Perth & Kinross Council has an ambitious plan to sweep away the 20th century entrance hall, along with the 1885 line, which is no longer required, and open up the view of the original station. This would also provide space for an adjacent bus station, so creating a convenient public transport hub. The key to this plan is, of course, finance. Sadly, altering railway lines, platforms and signalling is very expensive, and so far, nothing has happened.

The B-listed Station Hotel, on the north side of the station square, was built in 1890 to a design by Andrew Heiton Junior. It was once the premier hotel in Perth, with the largest and most prestigious ballroom, but its reputation has slipped in the last decade.

## The AK Bell Library

The AK Bell Library sits on a prominent site overlooking York

*Above right:*

Tudor-gothic tower and spire of Perth's Victorian station.

Queen Victoria's waiting room window, and the station clock, unchanged from 1870.

The Station Hotel.

### Trinity Church of the Nazarene

The large number of railway employees was important for Perth's economy and its society. The Church of the Nazarene, a Wesleyan nonconformist denomination, which was established in Perth in 1909, and recruited some of its most influential laymen from the railway fraternity. Since 1982 the congregation has used Trinity Church, an imposing building with twin slated spires looking across York Place to the AK Bell Library.

Twin spires of the Trinity church of the Nazarene. St John's spire can be seen in the distance.
MAP 1 · H8

The AK Bell Library.
MAP 1 · H7

Place, a little west of the old city wall. It was built originally as the Perth City and County Infirmary in 1836, and was the main hospital for the area, taking over the medical functions of the King James VI Hospital. The only surviving elements of the original building are the vaulted ceiling over the library entrance and the elegant A-listed neoclassical north block with its elaborate *porte cochère* built to protect patients from the elements as they arrived and departed from the hospital. After the opening of the new Perth Royal Infirmary in 1914, the building was used as a Red Cross centre during the First World War, then as a tuberculosis sanatorium, and thereafter as offices for the Local Authority.

In 1994, Perth & Kinross District Council converted the building into its main library, adding major extensions to the east and west faces of the old hospital, in what is rather disparagingly referred to as a 'post modern interpretation of classicism'. Whatever one's view of the architecture, the interior is spacious and full of natural light.

The Library houses Perth's extensive and justly famous Local Collection, which is much used for

**The AK Bell Library** commemorates three of Perth's famous sons. It is named after Arthur Kinmond Bell (see Chapter 5), whose Gannochy Trust made a large contribution to the building costs. The Soutar theatre, a well-appointed auditorium, honours the poet William Soutar (see Chapter 7). The Sandeman exhibition and meeting room is named after Professor Archibald Sandeman, who gifted Perth's first public library to the city (see Chapter 10).

genealogical and other research. It also has the extensive John McEwen archive and it hosts the Scots Language Resource Centre.

## Other Buildings in York Place

The Library Lodge, which sits forward from the library, was built in 1830 and refashioned in 1867. It was saved from demolition in 1999 and refurbished to become the headquarters of the Perth & Kinross Heritage Trust. Between the Library Lodge and the Library itself is the kinetic sculpture, *Wave* by Peter Fluck (1998), which is designed to reflect the unpredictable movement of wave and wind.

Opposite the Library Lodge on the corner of York Place and

Kinetic sculpture, *Wave*.

The Library Lodge.

John McEwen (1887–1992) was born near Aberfeldy, the son of a forester on the Garth Castle Estate. Schooling was unsuccessful and he left at 14 to start work as a forester in Aberdeenshire. Later he went to work in the Royal Botanic Gardens in Edinburgh, and then in the Glasgow Corporation Parks Department. These positions provided the opportunity to study, which he did voraciously, becoming a radical socialist. In 1920 he joined the newly created Forestry Commission where, two years later, he organised the setting up of a Trade Union. However, he was restless and moved to Ireland, and then back to Scotland, ending up in Perthshire as an independent forestry consultant. In 1961 he was elected to be the President of the Royal Scottish Forestry Society (only the second working forester to be so honoured). In 1963 he was awarded an OBE, and in 1980 was created a Fellow of the Royal Scottish Geographical Society.

In 1977, at the age of 90, he published his seminal work, *Who Owns Scotland?*, listing all the large (over 5,000 acres) estates in Scotland with their acreage, and demonstrating Scotland's uniquely concentrated land ownership pattern. He died just two days short of his 105th birthday.

The **Scots Language Resource Centre** seeks to record the written and spoken language of Scots, and promote it as one of Scotland's three official languages. Scots is now threatened, but was once universally used across the non-Gaelic speaking parts of the country, and it is still in common use today in playgrounds, at work, and within the family. While the administration of its Resource Centre is based in an office in the library, general access to the material is through its website: www.scotslanguage.com

Caledonian Road is a shop entrance which features an elaborate Edwardian Art Nouveau mosaic by GPK Young, designed in 1906.

No. 20 York Place is a mid-Victorian C-listed semi-detached villa. At the time of writing it is semi-derelict and fenced off, but it was once the manse of the Knox Free Church of Scotland, and the birthplace of John Buchan, the First Baron Tweedsmuir and a Freeman of the City of Perth. However, Buchan was only one year old when his father transferred to a new church in Kirkcaldy, and the family moved to Fife. At the time of writing, funds have recently been secured from the Perth City Heritage Fund to aid the restoration of this building.

Next door, at No. 22 York Place, is the headquarters of the Shetland Pony Stud Book Society – the oldest of the UK native breed societies.

**John Macnab by John Buchan**

Buchan's most famous novel after *The Thirty-Nine Steps*, is recalled on one of the pillars on the Tay Street floodwall, which shows the skeleton of a fish, and above it 'Mousetrap', which is the name of a salmon pool in the River Tay north of Dunkeld:

The novel tells the tale of three bored city gents, including a Cabinet Minister and ex-solicitor general who decide to turn to poaching. They issue a challenge to three Perthshire estates that surround the home of their host for the escapade. Of course, after some narrow escapes, they succeed, and their host marries the daughter of one of the estate owners. It is a story redolent of the aristocratic upstairs-downstairs society that inhabited Highland Perthshire before the Second World War.

Tay Street Pillar, recalls Buchan's novel *John Macnab*.

Art Nouveau shop entrance on the corner of York Place.
MAP 1 · H8

# CHAPTER THIRTEEN

# East of the Tay

SMALL SETTLEMENTS on the east bank of the Tay are as old as the City of Perth itself. They were clustered around the eastern end of the mediaeval bridge, the ford, and the jetties from which ferries crossed the river to Perth harbour.

In mediaeval times three small villages developed: Bridgend, Kinnoull, and Barnhill, but nothing of them now remains. Over the centuries the villages coalesced and they were officially incorporated into Perth after the opening of the Perth Bridge in 1772. Nevertheless, the community of Bridgend, Gannochy and Kinnoull (as it now calls itself) has thrived, and maintains a strong local identity.

The urban core of the built environment of the area is the Main Street of Bridgend with its tenements from the Georgian period now sadly dilapidated, and Strathmore Street. On the south side of Strathmore Street is a bronze sculpture by Frances Pelly (1976), of three human figures, one holding a bird, and above the figures three birds on the gable wall. Residential streets radiate from this core. Pitcullen Crescent leads north-east to Scone; Isla Road runs along the bank of the Tay to

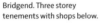

Bridgend. Three storey tenements with shops below.

Perth Bridge at night.

Bronze statues in Strathmore Street. Note the bronze birds on the gable wall.
MAP 2 · H4

Scone Palace; and Gowrie Street, which becomes the Dundee Road, heads south to Kinfauns and the Carse of Gowrie. This part of Perth is residential, with a broad mix of housing, varying from social rented apartments, to the Georgian and Victorian mansions on the bank of the Tay and the lower slopes of Kinnoull Hill. Nearer the top of the hill are the Gannochy Estate (see Chapter 5), the Murray Royal Hospital, and St Mary's Monastery. To the north is Moot Hill, Scone Palace and Perth Racecourse, and at the southern extremity, beneath the Friarton Bridge is the Perth base of Edrington Distillers, producers of The Famous Grouse.

## The Murray Royal Hospital

The Murray Royal mental hospital sits at the top of Lochie Brae at the western boundary of the City of Perth. The original Murray Royal, a solid, B-listed, Georgian complex of buildings, was designed by the Edinburgh architect William Burn. It was opened in 1827 and received its Royal Charter in the same year. With its wide open spaces and distant views, it was designed to be 'sufficiently secure to prevent injury or escape, but free from the gloomy aspect of confinement'. The regime was relaxed compared to the usual standards of the day.

In 2013 a completely new hospital

### James Murray

James Murray, the founder of the hospital was born in 1781 in humble but independent circumstances on a small holding on Moncreiffe Hill. His mother had an older son by a previous marriage, William Hope, who went to India where he amassed a considerable fortune. Weary of exile, William Hope and his family set off in 1809 to return to Scotland. Before he did so, however, he wrote a will leaving his fortune to his two half brothers, should he and his family perish. They sailed from Madras with a fleet of 16 Indiamen, but during a storm three of the ships foundered, with the loss of all crew and passengers, including the Hope family. James Murray's health was poor, and he did not live long to enjoy his fortune, dying in 1814. He had never married, and left the bulk of his estate for 'the purchase of ground and the erection of an Asylum for the reception of lunatic persons in the city of Perth and its neighbourhood'.

'Rohallion' the new Secure Care facility at the Murray Royal Hospital.

Stained-glass window by Douglas Strachan depicting the parable of the Good Samaritan.

Murray Royal Chapel.

costing £75m was opened by Alex Salmond, the First Minister. As well as state of the art facilities for local patients, a new 'medium secure unit' has been built. This is one of three such units in Scotland, which are delivering a new standard of care for patients who require to be confined but are considered not to be a serious risk to the public. This unit will cater for patients from the whole of the north and north-east of Scotland. The investment in this new hospital has guaranteed the long term future of the institution, and ensures Perth will play a very important part in Scotland's overall mental health provision. Sadly the neo-classical original hospital buildings are now disused and boarded up, and their future is uncertain.

The B-listed hospital chapel which lies between the original hospital and the new buildings, has been untouched by the development and will be retained by the NHS. It was designed by the physician superintendent, Dr AR Urquhart in 1903, and mostly built by the patients. It is a surprisingly large church, and features an apse behind the carved oak communion table and a stained-glass window by Douglas Strachan depicting the Good Samaritan. Over the entrance is a tower with an octagonal cupola.

## St Mary's Pastoral and Retreat Centre

'St Mary's Monastery', as it is known locally, was designed by Andrew Heiton Junior, and completed in 1870 for the Redemptorists' order. It occupies a prominent site near the top of Hatton Road on the slopes of Kinnoull Hill. It looks across the Tay

## The Walled Garden

The derelict walled garden in the grounds of the hospital was restored and developed to provide work for psychiatric patients, and ease their return to normal society. Now independent of the hospital and the NHS, it is run by a local charity, but still provides therapeutic work for psychiatric patients who live in the community. The garden is open daily, and there is a café and a shop for plants, vegetables and fruit.

A corner of the Walled Garden.

to St John's Kirk, from whence in 1559 the 'rascally mob' incited by John Knox surged across the town to sack the monasteries of the day. So Perth witnessed the start of Scotland's Reformation, but also the beginning of a new enlightened religious tolerance. For St Mary's was the first Roman Catholic religious house to be built in Scotland after the Reformation, and St Ninian's the first Episcopalian cathedral.

The monastery, a fine example of the neo-gothic revival of the 19th century, was built as a training centre for the priesthood. It is a very large building, four storeys high and with 60 rooms, which include a chapel, living quarters, lecture rooms, study areas, kitchens and a refectory. After 140 years the structure and living

## Building of the Monastery

Building work was fraught with difficulty, due to a hostile neighbour who diverted the local stream to deprive the monastery of water. Disaster loomed, but Divine help was to intervene. A monk digging in the garden struck a spring, from which a stream of water flowed. A shrine and a pool have been built at the source of this water, which is said to have healing properties. The stream is still flowing down Kinnoull Hill, passing through Bellwood Park, beside the newly planted heather collection, before entering the River Tay.

St Mary's Monastery.

Source of the 'Miraculous Stream' at St Mary's Monastery.
MAP 2 · H3

St Mary's Monastery Chapel.

quarters required to be refurbished and brought up to date. At the time of writing, work on the roof and exterior has been completed, and the internal refurbishment is progressing.

With the dearth of candidates for the priesthood, St Mary's has become an ecumenical residential centre for spiritual renewal, to serve the needs of people from Scotland and all over the world. The church is used weekly by the local Roman Catholic community, and the crypt, recently refurbished, is used as a meeting place by local organisations.

## Bowerswell House

No domestic property in Perth has featured more prominently in the city's social, artistic and civic history than Bowerswell House. The house itself, a fine Italianate villa, sits just above the Dundee Road off Bowerswell Road, and commands fine views to the west over the Tay and Perth. It was built between 1844 and 1877 on the site of an earlier house.

Bowerswell House.
MAP 1 · V11

### The Ruskin-Millais-Gray Triangle

The original Bowerswell House was the property of John Thomas Ruskin, the grandfather of the artist, author and prominent metropolitan art critic John Ruskin. Sadly John Thomas Ruskin committed suicide in the house in 1817, some ten days after the death of his wife. The house was later sold by his son, John James Ruskin, to George Gray, WS, a notable Perth lawyer, who was the father of 15 children, the eldest of whom was Effie, born in 1828.

The Ruskin and Gray families remained close and Effie and her sisters spent time with the Ruskin family in London, where she met John Ruskin, (the third) grandson of John Thomas. Effie was a very pretty girl, and in due course, in 1848, she and John Ruskin, who was nine years her senior, were married in Bowerswell House by the minister of Kinnoull Parish Church. The marriage, however, was not successful, was never consummated, and was eventually annulled in 1854 in a very high profile case, which scandalised Victorian society and has been, and is still, the subject of several theatre plays, books and films.

During this time Ruskin, who was at the height of his reputation as an author and art critic, had become involved with the young John Everett Millais, one of the founders of the Pre-Raphaelite Brotherhood. Ruskin appreciated Millais' talent and style and defended him against the hostile critics of the establishment. Millais' friendship with Ruskin introduced him to Effie and after they met she modelled for his painting *The Order of Release* (now in the Tate Gallery). During the sittings they fell in love. After the annulment of her marriage, Effie was married to Millais in 1855 in a cottage adjacent to Bowerswell House, by the (next) minister of Kinnoull Church. They had eight children.

Millais and Effie divided their time between London and Scotland, living for much of the time in Annat Lodge, high above Bowerswell, Effie's family home. Millais painted 21 large landscapes in Scotland. Sadly none of them are on view in Perth. However, as well as the portrait of Effie, the Museum and Art Gallery has one of his most famous works, *Waking*, a portrait of his daughter, Mary, sitting up in bed, probably in Annat Lodge. The gallery also possesses a portrait of Sir Robert Pullar, the Lord Provost of Perth. His most important work in Perth was the stained-glass west window of Kinnoull Church (see next page). Millais was created a Baronet in 1885, the first artist to be awarded a hereditary title. He died in 1896 and is buried in St Paul's Cathedral. Effie died the next year and is buried in the Kinnoull Aisle, just below Bowerswell House.

There are a number of prints of Millais' paintings in Bowerswell House, which is now owned by the Caledonia Housing Association. These include, *The Order of Release*, a famous winter scene, *Christmas Eve at Murthly Castle* (which

lies a few miles north of Perth), and *Bubbles*, used as an advertisement for Pear's soap.

The Gray family and Bowerswell were again prominent in the 1930s, when Melville Jameson Gray, Effie's younger brother by 19 years, and by then the owner of Bowerswell House was the instigator of the purchase of the 34 bells which form the carillon in the tower of St John's Kirk. Finally, in 1946, on the death of Melville Gray at the age of 99, Bowerswell House came on the market and was bought by the people of Perth to become a 'living memorial' to their dead of the Second World War.

Gravestone of Effie Gray and her 21-year-old son George in the Kinnoull aisle.
MAP 1 · T5

*Effie* by John Everett Millais.
© Perth Museum & Art Gallery, Perth & Kinross Council.

*Waking*, a portrait of the artist's daughter, Mary, by Millais.
© Perth Museum & Art Gallery, Perth & Kinross Council.

Floodlit Kinnoull church
across the Tay.
MAP 1 · T5

The Great West Window
by Sir John Millais.
© Louis Flood.

Flower motif.
© Louis Flood.

## Kinnoull Parish Church

By the early 1800s the population of
Bridgend and Kinnoull had increased
significantly, and the tiny Kinnoull
Parish Church was quite inadequate,
and also seriously dilapidated (see
Chapter 14). After many delays a new
church was built below Bowerswell
House on the Dundee Road, and
opened in 1827. The architect was
William Burn, who was at the same
time building the Murray Royal
Hospital. The church is built on a
Greek cross plan, and is lit by large
windows on all sides, so that inside it
is bright and airy. Many of the
windows are now embellished with
stained glass, including the Great East
Window by Douglas Strachan,
illustrating four important episodes in
the life of Christ, and a window
dedicated to the Boys' Brigade.

Most interesting, however, is the
five light Great West Window in the
chancel behind the communion table.
This window consists of 14 panels,
each illustrating one of the parables,
and 11 beautiful flower motifs. It was

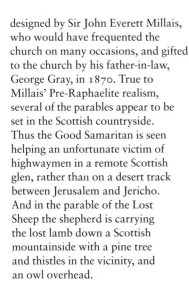

designed by Sir John Everett Millais, who would have frequented the church on many occasions, and gifted to the church by his father-in-law, George Gray, in 1870. True to Millais' Pre-Raphaelite realism, several of the parables appear to be set in the Scottish countryside. Thus the Good Samaritan is seen helping an unfortunate victim of highwaymen in a remote Scottish glen, rather than on a desert track between Jerusalem and Jericho. And in the parable of the Lost Sheep the shepherd is carrying the lost lamb down a Scottish mountainside with a pine tree and thistles in the vicinity, and an owl overhead.

# Moot Hill, the Stone of Destiny and Scone Palace

## Moot Hill – Silent Witness of Scottish History

Moot Hill, nowadays a fairly insignificant mound in the grounds of Scone Palace, was at one time at the epicentre of aristocratic and political life in Scotland. For two millennia it has watched the ebb and flow of Scottish history. The settlement around it, which became the mediaeval village of Scone, was the base for one of the more important local Pictish tribes. After the Romans withdrew south to Hadrian's Wall, this tribe gradually extended its authority over many of the war-lords and kinglets who controlled small patches of territory between Firth of Forth and the Pentland Firth, and eventually came to dominate

Pictland. In due course they embraced Christianity, and monks from Iona established a monastery in Scone in the seventh century.

When Kenneth MacAlpin defeated the Picts and killed their king in a battle near Scone in 843AD, he established himself as the first king of mainland Scotland, uniting the Scots from the west with the Picts in the east, and in doing so he created the first nation state in Europe. He brought with him the Stone of Destiny and the Gaelic traditions of Argyll, including especially the rituals associated with Dunadd, the rocky outcrop on the flat marshy plain near Loch Crinan, which was the hilltop coronation site, and centre of his kingdom of Dalriada. Moot Hill, though smaller than Dunadd, stood prominently above an escarpment overlooking the tidal marshes of the Tay. It must have seemed to him just the right place to set up the administration of his new kingdom. The name 'Moot' derives from the Old English word *mot* and the old Scots words *mut* or *mote*, all of which mean 'assembly' or 'meeting'. This is where MacAlpin and his successors presided over the affairs of the developing Kingdom of Scotland.

In 1114 the great Augustinian Abbey of Scone was founded by King Alexander I, and some time later the mediaeval village was elevated to the status of a Royal Burgh. However, while the Abbey of Scone provided occasional lodgings for the King, and a setting for ceremonies such as coronations, it was Perth that became the capital of Scotland, on account of its wealth, its harbour, its High Kirk and its civic buildings.

In 1559, during the Reformation, the Abbey was burned to the ground, and in due course the king gave the ruined buildings and land to William Ruthven of Huntingtower, who became the first Earl of Gowrie. His second son, the 3rd Earl, was fatally implicated in the Gowrie Conspiracy to assassinate King James VI in 1600 (see Chapter 9). As a result his palace and lands around Scone, were confiscated and given to the King's cup bearer, David Murray, who is the ancestor of the present Earl of Mansfield, who still lives in Scone Palace.

Moot Hill is now sadly diminished. It stands, a small green mound, capped by the Mansfield mausoleum, dwarfed by Scone Palace, and surrounded to the north and west by large trees. The Palace was built along the escarpment, so obscuring the view of the Hill from the Tay, and depriving it of its strategic and psychological importance.

Mausoleum on the top of Moot Hill, and replica Stone of Destiny.
MAP2 · G6

# The Stone of Destiny

Mounted on two short stone pillars in front of the Mansfield Mausoleum is a replica of the Stone of Destiny, the 'original' of which is in Edinburgh Castle. The setting is rather sad and plain for an object of such huge cultural importance.

So far as the Stone that is now in Edinburgh Castle is concerned, the verifiable facts begin in 1296, when Edward I of England surged through Scotland leaving a trail of death and destruction. On his way back from Montrose where King John Balliol had been captured, Edward sent a force to Perth to confiscate the Stone. It was taken, along with Scotland's crown, sceptre and sword of state, the Holy Rood of St Margaret (said to be a fragment of the true cross), and much else, to London, where the stone was incorporated into the throne in Westminster Abbey.

There it rested undisturbed until Christmas Eve, 1950, when a group

Tradition has it that King Kenneth MacAlpin brought with him from the west a polished black rock with mythical properties, on which were carved hieroglyphic letters and symbols. It was referred to in the 1800s as the 'Black Stone of Dunstaffnage' (a castle north of Oban). It was said to have been brought to Scotland from Egypt by a tribe descended from Pharaoh's daughter, Scota, which over a period of several hundred years had travelled via Spain to Ireland, and thence to Argyll. Whatever the origin of the Stone, it was certainly used for coronations and enthronements on Moot Hill for over 400 years, from around 860 until 1296 AD.

of nationalist students retrieved it in a daring raid. An enormous police operation was completely ineffective. For four months the Stone was missing, until in April, it was deposited in Arbroath Abbey, where the Declaration of Arbroath, Scotland's first Claim of Right, was signed in 1320. From there it was unceremoniously repossessed, and returned to Westminster.

In 1996, in an effort to appease the growing nationalist sentiment, it was brought back to Scotland and installed in Edinburgh Castle, beside the Honours of Scotland (the Crown, Sceptre and Sword of State). Later that year the composition of the stone was analysed, and there is no doubt that it came from the Kincarrathie sandstone quarry, about a mile from Scone Palace.

So what about the legend of the black stone with mythical properties and hieroglyphic carvings? The most likely explanation is that in 1296 the monks of Scone Abbey substituted a block of local sandstone for the real item when Edward's soldiers came looking for it. This would explain why it is so much smaller than similar mediaeval stone 'thrones' found elsewhere in Europe, and not black, or carved, and also why no efforts were made by King Robert the Bruce or later kings to get it back. They knew it was a substitute. The real mystery is the present whereabouts of MacAlpin's stone.

In spite of doubts about the authenticity of the stone in Edinburgh Castle, there are many in Perth who believe it should be returned to the City, and displayed either in Scone

Replica Stone of Destiny – definitely not the 'Black Stone of Dunstaffnage'.

Palace, or St John's Kirk, or the Museum and Art Gallery.

## Scone Palace

The Earls of Gowrie built the first Scone Palace, in the 1580s. It served them and then the Murray family until 1796, when David, the 3rd Earl of Mansfield, inherited the estate. He decided not to follow his father into public life, but to spend his time and money (lots of it) rebuilding the Scone family home as a magnificent Georgian gothic palace, enclosing a splendid regency interior, and setting it in appropriate parkland.

He engaged the architect William Atkinson to build his new palace on roughly the same footprint as its predecessor. And so, while elements of the mediaeval house have survived, in particular the dimensions of the Long Gallery, in essence the building we see today dates from 1812.

The A-listed palace is a long oblong structure, orientated roughly north to south, and built of red sandstone around a central courtyard, which is divided into two by the narrow Slip Gallery. Unusually, for a major gothic building, it is asymmetric.

The main southern element of the palace is built square like a fort, with battlements atop its three external sides, while the northern oblong part is more restrained, and is said to reflect the cloisters of the ancient Abbey of Scone.

The entrance to the palace is between two massive square towers on the east face of the 'fort'. Looking at the entrance, to the right are the windows of the Long Gallery, above the basement. To the left the state rooms of the palace occupy the corner of the building, and the south and west-facing aspects of the 'fort'. As the ground falls away, the basement windows of the west face are fully exposed, and the state rooms above command a magnificent view across flat parkland to the Tay, nearly a mile away, and over the river to Perth.

The entrance hallway leads into an inner reception area lit by a cupola, called the Octagon, which gives access to the state rooms and the Long Gallery. The Long Gallery – the longest room in Scotland at nearly 50 metres – has roughly the same dimensions as its mediaeval predecessor, and still has the original

Scone Palace from the south.
MAP2·G6

West face of Scone Palace, overlooking the River Tay.

marquetry floor. Its nine tall windows look out across the lawns to the mediaeval arch framing the ancient drive way approaching the palace, and to Moot Hill. Although the room was remodelled by Atkinson, its polished floor would have been familiar to James VI who was a regular visitor, and to Charles II who walked though the Long Gallery to his coronation on Moot Hill in 1651, nine years before he was crowned in London. It was also familiar to Queen Victoria and Prince Albert, who watched the Earl of Mansfield demonstrate the game of curling by 'throwing' a curling stone down its polished surface, as if it were ice. (see Chapter 15).

The formal rooms consist of the Inner Hall, the Ante-room, Dining Room, Drawing Room, Library and the Ambassador's Room. In addition there are the three rooms comprising Queen Victoria's suite, and the Lennox Room. These are arranged along the south and west sides of the 'fort'. They are beautifully decorated and lavishly furnished in Regency style with many items of great interest and value. The tour of the palace takes in all of these rooms, as well as the Long Gallery and Slip Gallery, and may include a visit to the tea-room and shop in the basement.

There is also the opportunity to wander in the surrounding park.

What distinguishes Scone Palace from many other great houses is that for the last four centuries it has been, and continues to be the Mansfield family home, and several senior members of the family are active in local business, artistic and social affairs. The palace has been used by Perth & Kinross Council for important events, such as the reception for Prince Charles, Duke of

Entrance to Scone Palace between two massive square towers.
© Perthshire Picture Agency/ Scone Palace.

The Long Gallery.
© Perthshire Picture Agency/ Scone Palace.

Prince Charles, Duke of Rothesay at Scone Palace to celebrate the 800th anniversary of Perth's Royal Charter.
Courtesy Angus Findlay.

Rothesay, when he visited Perth to celebrate the 800th anniversary of Perth's Royal Charter in 2010, and lunch for Her Majesty the Queen, when she came to Perth on the occasion of the restoration of City Status in 2012.

## Scone Palace Grounds

There is much to see in the extensive parkland that surrounds the palace, although there are no formal gardens. The topography of the policies divides the park into two separate parts. To the east and south of the palace is the site of the 'Royal Burgh of Scone', the palace stables, maze, pinetum and most of the woodland. To the west, below the escarpment there is a broad sweep of flat land between the palace and the Tay. While this area contains some important specimen trees most is used for grazing and for major events such as the annual Scottish Game Fair, and the hugely successful Rewind Concert. Perth Racecourse lies at its northern end.

**The Mausoleum:** The parish church, which stood on the top of Moot Hill, probably on the site of an early

Italian alabaster monument in the Scone Mausoleum.

Scone Mercat Cross.

Murray's landscape designer was John Loudon. His first task was to clear the ancient burgh from its location close to the palace, and relocate the 1,400 souls to a new site two miles to the east, which has developed into the thriving village of Scone. All that remains is the graveyard, the Mercat Cross, and the mediaeval arch facing the main entrance to the Palace. The arch was accidentally demolished by a lorry in 2011, but has been restored.

Culdee chapel, was almost completely demolished, except for part of the transept, which was retained and remodelled into the Mansfield mausoleum. Inside the mausoleum is a magnificent Italian alabaster monument by Maximillian Colt, commissioned by the first Viscount Stormont, and executed in 1618, nearly 200 years before the mausoleum was built. Around the mausoleum are a number of mature cedars of Lebanon, and a new one planted by Prince Charles.

**The Murray Star Maze:** Near the car park at the entrance to the palace grounds is the maze designed by contemporary maze designer Adrian Fisher. Designed in the shape of the heraldic symbol of the Murray family, a five-pointed star, it consists of 2,000 beech hedging plants, half of them green, and half copper, planted to give a tartan effect when viewed from above. In the centre of the maze is a fountain by sculptor David Williams-Ellis.

**The Pinetum and the David Douglas Pavilion:** In 1848 the 4th Earl established a pinetum of exotic conifers which is still being developed as new specimen trees are planted. It features avenues of wellingtonia, sitka spruce and noble fir. Information about David Douglas and the trees in Scone Palace grounds is displayed on a number of panels in the David Douglas pavilion, a shelter in the grounds between the palace and the pinetum.

One of the special trees is an enormous Douglas Fir, planted from seed collected by David Douglas in 1826. The Tree Council, in celebration of Her Majesty the Queen's Golden Jubilee in 2002, selected this tree to be, 'One of fifty great British trees, in recognition of its place in the national

heritage'. Another special tree is the King James VI sycamore, planted by the King on the escarpment quite close to the palace. Sadly, it is in an exposed position and was quite badly damaged in the storms of 2011. The Pinetum, and the individual specimen trees, form an important part of Perth & Kinross Council's Big Tree Country promotion, and was the location for the launch of the National Tree Collections of Scotland in June 2011.

## Perth Racecourse

The kings of Scotland and the people of Perth have enjoyed their racing for many centuries. Indeed in 2013 a

Murray Star Maze.
© Perthshire Picture Agency/
Scone Palace.

Fountain at the centre of the maze.

Plaque in front of the Douglas Fir in Scone Palace grounds.

David Douglas pavilion.

Tay Street pillar commemorating David Douglas.

### David Douglas

David Douglas was the most important of Scotland's great plant hunters. He was born the son of a stonemason in Scone in 1799, and on leaving school he served an apprenticeship as a gardener in the palace estate. After seven years at Scone he went to Valleyfield in Fife, where he was able to study botany and zoology in his spare time, and then to the Botanic Gardens of the University of Glasgow. There he impressed Professor William Jackson Hooker, who took him on botanical expeditions to the Highlands, and then recommended him to the Royal Horticultural Society of London.

The Society sent him on a number of plant hunting expeditions first of all to the north-west of America, from whence he sent back the seeds of many of his most important introductions – including the douglas fir, sitka spruce, lodgepole pine, noble fir and ponderosa pine. He also introduced a large number of other trees and plants including lupins, flowering currants, penstemon and the California poppy. In all, he is credited with introducing 240 new species of plants. He died at the age of only 36 in mysterious circumstances while on an expedition to Hawaii in 1834.

Douglas is commemorated on one of the pillars in the Tay Street floodwall. It shows a pineapple, which in form resembles a pinecone, and also relates to the location of his death in Hawaii. The text above, 'The wood began to move' is an excerpt from Shakespeare's *Macbeth*, and refers to Birnam Wood.

special race day was held to celebrate the 400th anniversary of the first record of racing in Perth, on the South Inch in 1613. In that year it is recorded that there was a contest for 'The' Silver Bell – the definite article indicating that racing in Perth was already an established sport.

In those days, races were held regularly on the Inches, first on the South Inch, and then from 1784 on the North Inch. Flat racing continued there until 1908, when the inaugural race meeting, under National Hunt Rules, was held on the present course in Scone Palace Park.

In recent years the course has developed steadily, with new stands and facilities, and further major developments are planned. Its beautiful setting and spectacular jumps attract the finest horses, trainers and jockeys on the circuit, giving Perth a reputation as a good testing ground for the season's high pressure races. It is generally considered to be the prettiest racecourse in Scotland, and has won many accolades, including the 'Best Smaller Racecourse in the North' seven times in the last decade. Attendance at race meetings has been rising sharply, making Perth the busiest racecourse in Scotland, and

The parade before the race.

bringing to the city an increasing share of Scotland's racing industry.

In between race meetings the facilities are well used as a distinctive venue for conferences, and other events.

### Museum of Racing

In 2013, to mark racing's 400th anniversary, a mobile museum of racing in Perth was set up called the History Horsebox Museum. This can be visited on race days in Perth, but more importantly, because it fits onto the back of a lorry, it can be taken to other venues, such as the Royal Highland Show, where it contributes an interesting exhibit, and a useful advertisement for racing in Perth.

Scone Mobile History Horsebox Museum.

CHAPTER FOURTEEN

# Perth's Parks and Green Spaces

PERTH IS FORTUNATE to have many areas of green space close to the city centre. Some of this land has been given to the people in perpetuity and may not be developed, and some of the rest consists of steep wooded slopes, which in the past were difficult to build on, and have now been protected.

The North Inch in winter. The Lynedoch Memorial is in the centre, and Rose Terrace behind.

Perth & District Pipe Band marches into the arena at the Highland Games.

## The North Inch

The North Inch is that wedge of land extending from the Perth Bridge and Charlotte Street along the west bank of the Tay for about a mile upriver. Gifted along with the South Inch to Perth by King Robert III in 1377, it was originally a marsh, but is now a grassy park, with mature trees around its perimeter. Over the centuries it has been used for golf, horse racing and other sports, and also for innumerable gatherings, from the Battle of the Clans in 1396 to Highland Games in modern times. It was a natural flood plain for the Tay. However, in 2000 the flood protection bank, built to defend the Muirton housing scheme, now protects the central area of the Inch, and gives it the appearance of an amphitheatre, making it well suited for major events.

Originally the land gifted by King Robert extended only as far as a ditch that ran from Balhousie Castle to the river. However, Thomas Hay Marshall arranged an exchange of land with the Earl of Kinnoull in 1795, which extended the park northwards, providing more space for golf, a curling pond and a new permanent racecourse.

In modern times, as well as golf and bowling, the regular sports taking place on the North Inch have been rugby, football and cricket.

However many other sports are played occasionally, including, for example, international tug of war championships and the largest international volleyball tournament in the UK.

## Bell's Sports Centre

In 1968 newspaper headlines told Perth's citizens that the Space Age had arrived, when the huge flying saucer shaped dome of Bell's Sports Centre was erected off Hay Street, on the edge of the North Inch. It was the biggest dome of its type in Europe at the time, and received a Civic Trust Award in 1970. Named after AK Bell, the centre has been extended and now provides a large indoor arena, badminton and squash courts, changing rooms for teams using the North Inch, a coaching centre and café all funded by the Gannochy Trust. It is an important facility for the whole of the east of Scotland, enabling Perth to stage regional and national championships in several indoor sports such as hockey, badminton and gymnastics.

Nearby on Hay Street, but quite separate, are the courts of Perth Tennis Club, founded in 1881, the oldest tennis club in Scotland.

## Balhousie Castle Museum

Next to Bell's Sports Centre and also overlooking the North Inch is Balhousie Castle. It was originally built in 1631 as an L-shaped tower house for the Hays of Kinnoull. In 1863 the 11th Earl of Kinnoull converted it into a castle in the Scottish Baronial style, with typical

crow-stepped gables and projecting towers.

Bell's Sports Centre.
MAP 2 · G4

During and after the Second World War, it served a number of military purposes, but it is now the HQ of the Black Watch Association and houses the Black Watch Museum. In 2008 the Association launched an ambitious appeal for £3.5m to buy the castle from the army, extend and redevelop it, and

Balhousie Castle.
MAP 2 · G4

Balhousie Castle and museum, with new extension and Copper Beech Café on the left.

The Empire Room in the refurbished museum.
© Courtesy of Black Watch Castle & Museum.

Statuettes of soldiers of the regiment by Charles Pilkington Jackson.
© Courtesy of Black Watch Castle & Museum.

equip it with modern facilities to conserve and display its priceless contents. These include the military records of all Black Watch soldiers and more than 3,000 artefacts and memorabilia pertaining to the Black Watch for the last 250 years – medals, uniforms, weapons, trophies of war and some magnificent paintings. The appeal was successful and the refurbished museum was opened in 2013. It includes a café-restaurant, the Copper Beech Café, a hall for lectures, and modern exhibition rooms. Among the

exhibits are a group of statuettes, each about 15 inches high, designed in the late 1920s by the leading Scottish sculptor, Charles d'Orville Pilkington Jackson, the sculptor who created the Bruce statue at Bannockburn. Each shows a soldier of the Regiment at a different point in its history.

## The South Inch

The other part of the gift of King Robert III to Perth, the South Inch, is a square plot of park land, to the south of the city, overlooked by Marshall Place and St Leonard's Bank. It is bisected by the Edinburgh road, which divides it into two very different areas.

The main part, to the west of the road, is a grassy park, criss-crossed by tree-lined walkways. Look carefully, however, and note how it has become an integral part of Perth's flood defence scheme. Around its perimeter are flood banks that look so natural they escape notice. Their purpose is to enable the park to be used, in an emergency, as a huge pond, several feet deep, to defend the

southern part of the city. A structure that looks like a group of standing stones adjacent to the Edinburgh Road conceals valves and a culvert leading to powerful pumps, which control the water level. At the western edge of the park, at its highest level

and protected from flooding, are a boating pond, a children's play area and other facilities.

Spring bulbs line the cycle and foot paths on the South Inch.

Perth's 'Standing Stones' hide the valves that control the water level in times of flood.
MAP 2 · G2

### The Black Watch at Bay: The Battle of Quatre Bras

This famous painting by William Barnes Wollen hangs in the Copper Beech Café. It depicts the desperate, but victorious, stand by the Black Watch in the battle that was the turning point in Wellington's campaign against Napoleon, allowing him to move on and triumph at Waterloo a few days later.

*The Black Watch at Bay. Battle of Quatre Bras* by Barnes Wollen.
© Black Watch Castle & Museum.

The annual two-day Perth Show takes place on the South Inch, beginning on the first Friday in August.

To the east of the Edinburgh Road is the Lesser South Inch. This contains a substantial area of hard standing, which is used for parking, fun fairs, circuses etc, and a large and very well used skate park. It was once the site of Cromwell's Citadel.

# The Citadel

Built by Oliver Cromwell after he captured Perth in 1651, the citadel was an enormous structure, 244 meters square, surrounded by a moat 30 meters wide. It could house 1,000 soldiers and 200 horses. It was strategically located adjacent to the river, with its north-eastern corner where the Fergusson Gallery now stands so that its guns controlled access to the town from the south and east and overlooked the river. Building the citadel caused immense damage to Perth. The burgh's main school, the hospital, 140 houses and the market cross were all demolished, and 200 tombstones from Greyfriars Burial Ground were removed to provide building material.

## Moncreiffe Island

This pear-shaped, flood-prone island is about a mile long and lies in the middle of the river with its apex level with Canal Street. The main branch of the river flows down its west side, then turns through 90 degrees round the base of the island, to head eastwards towards the North Sea. The island was part of the Moncreiffe Estate, and for many years filter beds for cleansing Perth's water supply were located at its northern end. In 1888 the Council bought the island to enable the filter beds to be enlarged to cope with Perth's expanding need for clean water.

Historically, the island could be reached only by the causeway from the east bank. This remains the only vehicular access, but it is passable only at low tide and when the river is low. However, in 1895 a stairway was built leading from the railway walkway down to the island. The

council then leased six acres for ground to the Perth Working Men's Garden Association for allotments (which still exist), and the southern part of the island to the King James VI Golf Club for a new private golf course. Public access to the island was guaranteed in the various rental agreements, and the island continues to be popular with walkers.

## Golf in Perth

The first record of golf in Scotland appears in 1457 in an Act of the Scottish Parliament forbidding golf in favour of archery. Similar edicts were repeated in 1471 and 1491, but in none of these did it state where the golf was being played. However, in 1502, the royal accounts record that King James IV bought clubs and golf balls in Perth – making him the first named golfer, and Perth the first named place in the world to be identified with the game. Perth could justify a claim to be the home of golf.

## The Royal Perth Golfing Society

This was set up as the Perth Golfing Society in 1824, and was immediately successful in attracting all the right

establishment people to its membership. Nine years later, in 1833, this paid off handsomely. The Captain of the Society, Lord Kinnaird, was in London, and as he reported to members, 'took the opportunity of addressing a letter to His Majesty King William the Fourth, asking him to become a patron of the Society, and asking him to grant his permission for styling it in future THE ROYAL PERTH GOLFING SOCIETY'. Remarkably, the king agreed, making the Perth Society the first golf club in the world to get royal patronage. The Society of St Andrews Golfers, which was much older and was stung, no doubt, by Perth's insouciance, requested and received royal patronage in 1836, and became the Royal and Ancient Golf Club in 1897.

At first the Society played much of its golf on the South Inch – a game being twice round the eight holes! In 1835 they moved to the larger 10-hole course on the North Inch. They shared the ground with the racecourse, and right up to the 1850s the Inch could be closed from May to September to allow the citizens of Perth to graze their cattle! The Society's clubrooms are at No 1. Atholl Crescent.

## The King James VI Golf Club and The Perth Artisan Golf Club

In 1858, a split developed in the Royal Perth Golfing Society and a new club was formed, called The King James VI Golf Club, in recognition of the fact that James VI was well known to have learned to play golf in Perth. Nevertheless, both clubs continued to use the North Inch course, now enlarged to 12 holes. In 1879 yet another club was formed, The Perth Artisan Golf Club. It continues today and has clubrooms overlooking the second tee of the North Inch course.

## Perth's Golf Courses

Perth has three golf courses within the city boundary. The North Inch course is owned by the City of Perth. The Island Golf Course and the Craigie Hill courses are private, owned by their members, and both have excellent club facilities. Visitors are welcome to play on all the courses.

### The North Inch Golf Course

Beasley's *World Atlas of Golf* asserts that in 1803, the six-hole course on the North Inch was the first recognisable golf course in the world. Golf was at that time, however, not what it is now. The first lawnmower was invented in 1830, and before that the only way to keep a good sward on the fairways and greens was to graze sheep or cut the grass with a scythe. The course was enlarged in stages, eventually in 1892 to 18 holes, under the direction of 'Old' Tom Morris of St Andrews.

### The King James VI Course

When regular access to the island was made possible by the stairway from the railway bridge, the officials of the King James VI Club petitioned the Council to grant the Club a lease for the main part of the island in order to construct a private golf

course. This was accepted, and 'Old' Tom Morris was brought, once again, from St Andrews to design the course. It was opened on 19 June 1897. In due course the clubhouse was built on a concrete plinth, to raise it above the flood plain. The downside of the inaccessible location is emergency access. In 1955 the clubhouse caught fire, and by the time the fire brigade had manhandled a small auxiliary pump across the bridge it had burned down completely, destroying everything within it. However, a new more modern clubhouse was built the next year.

The King James VI Golf Course is a jewel in Perth's crown, and a unique asset for the City. It is the

Bunkered in front of the 16th green of the North Inch course.

Clubhouse of the King James VI Golf Club.
MAP 1 · S1

King Jimmy's Cider.

18th green and clubhouse on the Craigie Hill Golf Course. MAP 2 · E1

Sculpture 1 *Bud* with 'Fortune' on the base. Vandalised and broken.

Sculpture 2 on plan. *Vortex.*

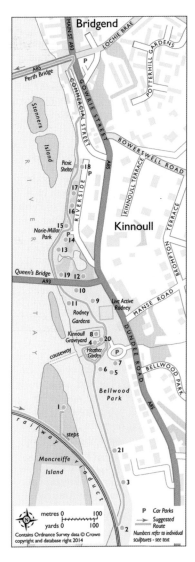

only golf course in the world that is within walking distance of the city centre; accessible only by foot; entirely contained on an island; and designed by Tom Morris.

The inaccessible location also hampers the harvesting of the apples from five big old apple trees on the island – three by the 5th green and two by the 12th. In a good year over two tons of apples are transported across the river and taken to the Cairn o' Mohr winery, ten miles east of Perth, in the Carse of Gowrie. There they are used to produce a special 'edition' of cider, named with typical irreverence, King Jimmy's Cider.

**Craigie Hill** is Perth's third golf course. Opened in 1911, it is completely different from the flat North Inch and Island courses. Constructed on the side of Craigie Hill, it is an energetic course to play, but affords spectacular views over Perth to the Sidlaw Hills, and north up the Tay Valley to the Grampian Mountains.

# Riverside Park

Riverside Park is the narrow strip of land that extends along the east bank of the Tay from the Railway Bridge almost as far as the Perth Bridge. It consists of (from south to north) Bellwood Park, the Kinnoull Aisle and churchyard, Rodney Gardens, and to the north of the Queen's Bridge, the Norie-Miller Park. Scattered throughout the whole park are modern sculptures of different sizes and subjects – some humorous, others enigmatic, some reflective, others practical, and some commemorative. They add interest to a pleasant walk through the gardens along the bank of the river and are numbered on the accompanying map. Riverside Park and the Sculpture Trail are best appreciated by crossing the Tay on the walkway beside the railway bridge, and entering the southern end of Bellwood Park.

## Bellwood Park

This is the surviving fragment of Bellwood Nurseries, once a 60-acre market garden and nursery. It was established in 1766 and thrived for over 100 years, during which time it developed some notable plants. Most famous of these were the Double Scotch Roses, bred from a wild rose found on Kinnoull Hill, above the nursery. The Scarlet Hawthorne was also bred here, and the nursery introduced the Swedish turnip, the Swede, to Britain. The park is leased to the Council by the Gannochy Trust.

### *Bud, Leaf* and *Seed*

The Sculpture Trail (see map on p. 162) begins at the stairway onto the railway bridge walkway at the southern end of Tay Street. Halfway across the bridge, descend the steps to the Island, where the first item on the trail is to be found at its northern tip close to the causeway. It is the first of a group of three enigmatic

sculptures inspired by the writings of Sir Patrick Geddes, and created by David Wilson in 1988. It is 'Bud', with 'Fortune' inscribed on the base (No. 1 on the map), but sadly it has been vandalised, and the bronze bud is missing.

From the end of the Railway Bridge, on the east bank of the river, there is a path through Riverside Park, leading northwards beside the river. The first sculpture on the trail is the uninspiring concrete 'Vortex' (No. 2 on the map), by Malcolm Robertson (1994). A short distance along the path is the second of David Wilson's group (No. 3) 'Leaf', with 'Insight' on the base. The third one, 'Seed', with 'Reason' on the base (No. 4) is further along the path by the Heather Garden.

As the walker approaches the Old Kinnoull Kirkyard, there is a grassy bank on the right on which is 'River Arch' (No. 5), by Doug Cocker (1998), representing the river and its bridges. Close by is 'Millais' Viewpoint' (No. 6), by Tim Shutter (1997). It is situated on what is said to be one of Millais' favourite spots overlooking the Tay. It consists of the lower part of a huge, heavily moulded picture frame, on which is sculpted falling leaves. This recalls one of Millais' most famous pictures – 'Autumn Leaves', painted in Perth, but now in Manchester City Art Gallery. This sculpture literally 'frames' the view of Perth with the spires of St John's and St Matthew's Kirks. Nearby, adjacent to the car park is the Rivers Race (No. 7) picnic spot, designed by Valerie Pragness, in 1997.

Sculpture 3. 'Leaf' with 'Insight' on the plinth.

Sculpture 4. 'Seed' with 'Reason' on the plinth.

Sculpture 5. 'River Arch'.

## The Heather Garden

Alongside the path and on the banks of the stream that runs down Kinnoull Hill from St Mary's Monastery is Perth's Heather Garden ('H' on the map). This has been a feature of Perth's horticulture for

many years and now has nearly 1,000 heather varieties. The garden has been moved recently from its previous location to Bellwood Park, and the opportunity has been taken to refresh it, and add a number of new varieties to ensure that it continues to be an important National Collection.

## Kinnoull Aisle: The Old Kinnoull Church and Graveyard

In the centre of Riverside Park is the walled graveyard ('K' on the map) surrounding the 'Kinnoull Aisle'. This is the only remaining element of the pre-Reformation church dedicated to St Constantine, which had served the Kinnoull Parish since at least 1287. An event took place in this church in 1515 that underscored the local importance of the church adjacent as it was to both Scone and Perth, and the national importance of Perth in Scotland. It was the wedding of Archibald Douglas, the Sixth Earl of Angus, to Margaret Tudor, the young widow of James IV who had been killed at Flodden, and the sister of King Henry VIII of England. Archibald Douglas was the nephew of Gavin Douglas, Bishop of Dunkeld who may have officiated at the wedding. This union was to have important consequences for the crown of Scotland, for it cemented the claim of James VI to the English throne. Margaret Tudor's son by her first marriage was James V, the father of Mary Queen of Scots, while her daughter by the Earl of Angus was the mother of Henry, Lord Darnley, Mary's husband. James VI was thus

## Sir George Hay, First Earl of Kinnoull 1572–1634

George Hay was a remarkable man. Born the fourth son of Sir Peter Hay of Megginch, which lies to the east of Perth, he was a shrewd entrepreneur, a clever administrator and an ambitious social climber. He was present at the Gowrie Conspiracy in 1600, and was rewarded for his loyalty to the king with lands confiscated from the Earl of Gowrie. He was knighted in 1609, elevated to the peerage in 1627, as Viscount Dupplin, and under Charles I, became Earl of Kinnoull in 1633. He was Lord Chancellor of Scotland from 1622 to 1633, and Keeper of the Great Seal.

Hay's main claim to fame as an entrepreneur was the first patent to manufacture glass in Scotland, which he received from King James VI in 1609. He established his factory on the shores of Loch Maree on the west coast, where there was a sheltered harbour, a plentiful supply of sand, and wood for charcoal.

### Glass Manufacture in Perth

No one in Perth pursued Sir George's patent, but 250 years later glass manufacture was established in Perth and became a very important industry. It began with the production of gauge glass for the steam boilers used in railway locomotives and ships. These gauges were subjected to very high pressures and temperatures, and had to be replaced frequently. There was a big market locally because of the railway repair workshops, but the gauges were also exported worldwide.

In the 1920s the Spanish master glass maker, Salvador Ysart joined the Perth firm, and led its diversification into decorative glass. For more than half a century the Ysart family, father and three

descended from the English crown through both his father and mother. (On her death, Margaret Tudor was buried in the Carthusian monastery. See Chapter 12).

Old Kinnoull Parish Church was demolished in 1824 when the new church was built a few hundred yards up river. Now all that remains is the side aisle, which became the mausoleum for the Earls of Kinnoull. It contains the monument to Sir George Hay, the first Earl of Kinnoull (No. 8 on the map of the Sculpture Trail). This has been a magnificent monument, worthy of a man of his achievements, but it has weathered significantly and is in need of some restoration, and is very poorly displayed.

Modified Davy lamp used to transport the Olympic Flame by air.

sons, played an enormous role in glass manufacture, making Perth the centre of glass making in Scotland. They produced the Monart (1930s and 40s) and Vasart (postwar) ranges of decorative glass, which became very fashionable and are now much sought after collectors' items. In 1962 Paul Ysart moved to Caithness Glass in Wick, where he specialised in paperweights. Later production moved back to Perth, and now continues in Crieff.

The production of industrial glass still continues in Perth at Spectraglass, from whence gauges for steam boilers and the petrochemical industry, are still exported world wide. One of their more unusual contracts is the production of a special glass cylinder for modified Davy lamps which are used to transport the Olympic Flame (which must never go out), whenever it travels by air on its tour around the world prior to the games. The contract for four Davy lamps has been renewed at every Olympic Games since the Winter Olympics at Lake Placid in 1980, and has already been signed for Rio de Janeiro in 2016.

Gravestone for Robert Knox, boatman from Bridgend, and his wife, Agnes Boyd.

Back of the Robert Knox/ Agnes Boyd gravestone.

Gravestone of Mary Duff, boatwoman, 1782.

Surrounding the aisle is the (A-listed) old churchyard, which contains a number of interesting headstones. Three are of particular note. The Robert Knox stone, dated 1708, is still very legible, and on the reverse shows a cherub, a simple boat on the water and the initials RK AB. The Mary Duff stone, dated 1782, is more unusual. It has a skilfully carved boatwoman, watched over by an angel, on the reverse of the stone –

one of very few early stones depicting a woman. The third is the grave stone of Effie Gray or Millais, which is affixed to the wall of the aisle.

# Rodney Gardens

Beyond the Kinnoull Aisle are the well-manicured Rodney Gardens, in front of the Live Active Rodney Pavilion, now a fitness centre ('R' on the map). Two sculptures in this part of the park are worthy of particular attention. 'Evergreen' (No. 9) is a tribute to Sir Patrick Geddes by Kenny Munro (1998). It is a tall structure of Corennie granite, marble and bronze surrounded by a garden. The finial, words, images and the garden all allude to Geddes's environmental thinking. The second sculpture (No. 10), a bronze by wildlife artist David Annand, is 'Foxtrot Ridge' (1992). On the approach to the causeway across to the island is a new work (No. 11), Bothy Boats by Kenny Munro (2012), which celebrates Perthshire's landscape.

### Sir Patrick Geddes 1854–1932

Patrick Geddes was born in Aberdeenshire, but came grew up in Perth in Mount Tabor Cottage, which sits above Rodney Gardens. Here he had an opportunity to walk in the woods of Kinnoull Hill, observe the wildlife, and also look out over the Royal Burgh of Perth and note its regular street plan. His upbringing in Perth greatly influenced his later environmental thinking.

He attended Perth Academy, and then studied in London under Thomas Henry Huxley, the noted proponent of Darwin's theory of evolution. He returned to Scotland and lectured in Zoology in Edinburgh University, before taking the Chair of Botany in Queen's College, Dundee, which he held for 25 years. Here he developed his pioneering ideas in biology, sociology and urban planning. He then became professor of Civics and Sociology in Bombay.

Geddes's innovative thinking and his ability to relate biological and sociological observations to urban planning earned him the title of 'The Father of Town Planning'. He coined the term 'conurbation' and the phrase, 'Think Global, Act Local'.

Geddes was also a great Francophile, and founded The Scots College in Montpellier.

Sculpture 9. *Evergreen*. Tribute to Patrick Geddes.

Sculpture 10. *Foxtrot Ridge*.

Sculpture 11. *Bothy Boats*.

Mount Tabor Cottage, now called Gean Tree Cottage, the childhood home of Sir Patrick Geddes.
MAP 2 · H3

## Norie-Miller Park

From the Rodney Gardens, two underpasses lead the pedestrian beneath the Queen's Bridge to the Norie-Miller Park, gifted to the people of Perth by Sir Stanley Norie-Miller. Here weeping willows trail their branches into the river where once ferryboats plied the river from the 'Gibralter' (spelled with an 'e') quay. This connection is recorded on one of the pillars on the Tay Street floodwall opposite. The design represents the prow of a boat, and the 'bees' on it are the 'busy bees', which were the river ferry boats.

The park is enlivened by two duck ponds at different levels, which are fed by a stream that cascades down from Kinnoull Hill. Near the upper pond is an uninspiring stainless steel sculpture, 'Blooming Lovely' (No. 12) by Richard Powell (1998), representing a domestic table with flowers on it. Farther along the riverbank, 'Benchmark' (No. 13) by John Creed (1998) is the easiest to understand. It consists of a series of wood and metal benches extending down the bank towards the river, representing the power of the river and tide, and flood levels reached by the Tay. Farther up the bank is 'The

Willow trees in Norie-Miller Park, at the site of the Gibralter dock.

Tay Street pillar, *Gibralter*, on the Tay Street floodwall.

Sculpture 12. *Blooming Lovely*.

Dance Within' (No. 14) by Paul Eugene Riley (1998), a large copper impregnated resin structure, representing a totem poll, and symbolising the rhythms of life. Nearby, facing the car park, is a 1972 bas-relief of Sir Stanley Norie-Miller (No. 15) by the Dundee sculptor, Scott Sutherland, whose best known work is the Commando Memorial at Spean Bridge.

In the most northerly section of the park there is a huge sundial (No. 16) by the Lovejoy Partnership

(1970), now quite overshadowed by trees. Nearby is 'Two Buoys Playing', (sic) (No. 17) by Chris Biddlecombe (1997), which is said to be a

contemplative work, and a metaphor for music and storytelling beside the river. Finally, there is an unfathomable piece of sculpture, like a huge gravestone, with 'CONSIDER' inscribed on one Side and 'BELOVED' on the other. It is called the 'Thought Stone', (No. 18) and is by Donald Urquhart (1998).

Scattered through the park are three triploid litter bins (19, 20, 21 on the map) by Phil Johnson (1998), decorated by galvanised steel representations of grasses. These give the bins height, so they can be seen from a distance. At the end of the walk is a substantial picnic shelter, a gift to Perth by the United States arm of the General Accident Corporation.

## Commercial Street

From the Norie-Miller Park the footpath leads across Commercial Street to the east end of the Perth Bridge, and back to Tay Street. This was once the site of an important part of Perth's shipbuilding industry, but was seriously flood-prone, and by the mid-20th century had become derelict. It was rebuilt between 1975 and 1978, as an irregular group of houses and flats with peaked roofs, sandblasted pink concrete walls and traditional windows overlooking the river. In 1980 it was awarded Civic Trust and Saltire Society Awards.

## Branklyn Garden

Lying above and to the east of Bellwood Park is Branklyn Garden, 'the finest two acres of private garden in the country', as one expert said. It is now owned by the National Trust

*Opposite page, above right:*
Sculpture 13. *Benchmark*.

Sculpture 14. *The Dance Within*.

Sculpture 16. *Sundial*

*Top left:*
Sculpture 18. The south face of the *Thought Stone*.

Sculptures 19, 20 and 21. Galvanised litter bin.

The Picnic Shelter.

*Above right:*
Sculpture 17. *Two Buoys Playing*.

Sculpture 15. Bust of Sir Stanley Norie-Miller BT, MC, DL, JP.

Commercial Street.
MAP 1 · T12

Himalayan blue poppy, in
Branklyn garden.
MAP 2 · H2

Pillar Sculpture: Blue Kinnoull.
The Meconopsis species from
Branklyn Garden.

Forrest, Frank Ludlow and George
Sherriff, were closely associated with
Branklyn and regularly sent plants
and seeds to the Rentons. In the
1930s George Sherriff sent the
Rentons the first seeds of the
Himalayan blue poppy, *Meconopsis*,
which is the flower now most
associated with Branklyn. A National
Collection of *Meconopsis*, consisting
of five different species (not all of
them blue) and 25 cultivars is now
held by Branklyn. One of them, the
'Blue Kinnoull', is represented on a
pillar on Tay Street's flood protection
wall. The Rentons pioneered the use
of peat blocks to build banks and
garden retaining walls. Peat provides
a moist, well drained, acid
environment which is particularly
suitable for many Himalayan plants.

Branklyn also holds a National
Collections of *Lilium*, the true 'lily',
of which there are around 110
species, *Rhododendron taliense*, a
hardy dwarf growing species of
Rhododendron, and *Casiope*, a
species of heather native to the arctic.
There is also a large collection of
primulas, many of which were
sourced from the Himalayas.

for Scotland and is open to all. It is a
garden of amazing density, with over
3,500 different species of flowers,
shrubs and trees. John and Dorothy
Renton bought the ground in the
1920s and built on it a beautiful arts
and crafts house (visible, but not
open to the public) and, over the next
40 years, developed a garden of
international acclaim, specialising in
Himalayan flora.

In the 19th and early 20th
centuries Scotland produced some of
the world's most important plant
hunters. Three of them, George

## Countryside Walks in Perth

Perth lies in a hollow and is
surrounded by low hills that offer
excellent walking, spectacular views,
and much else of interest.

### Kinnoull Hill, Deuchny Wood and Binn Hill

Above Branklyn Garden, a broad
stretch of Forestry Commission
woodland covers the slopes of three

low hills – Kinnoull Hill, Deuchny Hill and Binn Hill – and extends for two miles along the top of the cliffs overhanging the A90 Perth to Dundee

road. There are approximately 25 miles of way-marked paths which are ideal for walking, cycling and riding, and there is much to see. Access can be gained past the Branklyn Garden gate, and from car parks at Corsie Hill and Muirhall Road.

From the top of Kinnoull Hill (222 meters) there is a 360-degree panoramic view taking in the Lomond Hills in Fife, Ben More to the west above Crianlarich, Lochnagar in the Grampians, and the Tay estuary to the east. A little below the summit is the Kinnoull Tower, a folly sitting on top of one of the most prominent ramparts of the cliff. It was built as a replica of the outlook towers along the Rhine Valley by Lord Hay of Kinnoull in 1829. There is another tower near the top of Binn Hill, farther east. It was built by Lord Gray of Kinfauns in 1813, probably as an observatory. Although much larger, it is not so prominent as the Kinnoull tower, but it is visible from the A90.

In the 1920s, part of Deuchny wood was planted with exotic

*Above:*
Viewpoint at summit of Kinnoull Hill. Schiehallion is in the distance.

*Top left:*
The folly on Kinnoull Hill in autumn.
MAP 2·12

Tower folly on Binn Hill.

A winter scene at Quarrymill
Woodland Park.
MAP 2 · G5

Golfers on the Craigie Hill
Golf Course. Spire of St John's
Kirk in the distance.
MAP 2 · E2

conifers, including some magnificent
Wellingtonias. Nearly a century later,
a generous bequest from James Aitken,
an influential landscape gardener in
Perth, has enabled the area to be
developed by the Perth & Kinross
Countryside Trust and the Forestry
Commission as an arboretum, with
many new plants. It is now
incorporated into the Countryside
Trust's Big Tree Country scheme.

## Quarrymill Woodland Walks

The Annaty Burn cascades down
over many small waterfalls and two
mill ponds from the Den of Scone,
near Scone Old Parish Church, to
reach the Tay about a mile up river
from the Perth Bridge. Waterwheels
powered the machinery in the nearby
quarry, where sandstone was
extracted for Perth's bridges, and St
John's Kirk. There is a car park

adjacent to the A92, from which
way-marked paths follow both sides
of the burn. During the summer
months there is an excellent tea-room
adjacent to the car park, the profits
going to Macmillan Cancer Support.

## Craigie Hill, Mailer Hill and Moncreiffe Hill

On the other side of the Tay, the hills
to the south of Perth afford
spectacular views. Way-marked paths
fan out from the Moncreiffe car park
and from Cherrybank. The excellent
Cherrybank Inn used to be the centre
of a small clachan beside Perth's main
route to the south-west, but it is now
incorporated into Perth. The
landscaped Craigie Hill Golf Course
contrasts with the open pasture of
the upper part of the hill. The M90
can be crossed safely in two places to
reach Mailer Hill (182 metres), the

highest point in the area. Moncreiffe Hill, which lies opposite Kinnoull Hill to the west of the A90, is outwith the borders of Perth, but affords magnificent views over the city. A way-marked path is signposted from the unclassified Rhynd Road, which can be reached from Bridge of Earn.

## Angling on the Tay

The Tay is the premier salmon-fishing river in Scotland, and one of the great salmon rivers in the world.

Net fishing on the Tay dates back many centuries, with exports of salt fish in barrels going to ports in Europe from the Baltic to the Mediterranean. With the coming of the railway, and the ability to send fresh fish in ice to the major markets in the English cities, the business boomed to unsustainable levels. The Tay Salmon Fisheries Company was formed in 1899 in an effort to manage the industry gradually bought up all the netting stations on the river. It became the largest inshore fisheries company in Europe, with its own railway sidings, and an ice house adjacent to the station. In the 1980s and 1990s, however, for reasons that are not understood, fish numbers crashed and in 1987 the Tay Foundation, a charitable trust committed to the conservation of fish stocks and the aquatic environment, was established. It gradually took over, and closed down all the Tay netting stations. The last nets were pulled in 1996.

Rod fishing from the riverbank and from boats, however, continues to thrive, especially with 'catch and release' and is very important for the

Fishing from a boat up-stream from Perth.

Angling below the Perth Bridge.

economy of the whole of Perthshire. It can be very expensive, but the Perth Common Good Fund owns the fishing rights on the west bank of the river from the North Inch to the Friarton Bridge, and on some other smaller stretches of riverbank, on both sides of the river. Daily permits for visitors are very reasonable

Willowgate Trout Fishery.
MAP 2 · H1

indeed. Residents of Perth and Kinross can purchase seasonal permits, which also include the right to fish from Moncrieffe Island.

**The Willowgate Trout Fisheries** are nine acres of artificial ponds that have been constructed on the site of one of the netting stations on the east bank of the river, just beneath the Friarton Bridge. It is regularly stocked with rainbow trout, which may be fished with fly only. Tickets to fish the ponds can be purchased from the bothy, which used to service this particular station. It has been carefully restored, and features a café with a woodburning stove.

Willowgate can be reached by a signposted path along the riverbank from the end of the railway bridge walkway. It is quite tough going, but particularly interesting because it passes through one of the old orchards for which this part of Scotland was famous. Vehicular access to Willowgate is off the slip road at the Friarton interchange.

# CHAPTER FIFTEEN

# Perth's Suburban Arc

From the South Inch, Perth's suburban developments sweep west and north, encircling the heart of the city before returning to the Tay at the North Inch. Most of this area was built up in the late 19th and 20th centuries, and is a mix of modern residential, commercial and civic developments. In the process, some much older buildings that were once on the outskirts of the city and others which were surrounded by open country have become integral parts of Perth itself.

## Southern Approaches

In mediaeval times, the route to Edinburgh left Perth from the South Port or gate at the western end of South Street, and proceeded along the edge of Craigie Hill, avoiding the soft marshland of the South Inch (see Roy's Military Map, p. 187). However, by the mid-18th century, the South Inch was adequately drained and the Edinburgh Road was built across it, bringing more traffic (especially stagecoaches) right into the heart of Perth.

## Perth Prison

Perth's prison has been, and is still, important for the city's economy, although it is hardly on the tourist itinerary. Nevertheless, parts of it are A-listed, and it occupies a prominent site adjacent to the South Inch, with its main gate opening onto the Edinburgh Road. The original prison was designed by Robert Reid, and built in 1811 with a high wall, a moat, and defences to protect against attack from the inside! Its purpose was to house 7,000 French prisoners of war, at a time when Perth's population was about 20,000. However, it became redundant after the end of the Napoleonic Wars, and was reconstructed in the mid-19th century to become the General Prison for Scotland for all convicts serving nine months or more. Over the last 150 years there have been many changes, and it is still an important penal establishment.

## Perth Harbour

As plans to build Tay Street gathered pace in the 1840s, harbour

Perth Prison.
MAP 2 · G2

Perth harbour.
MAP 2 · G1

The 'Fair Maid', Perth's harbour tender.

Cargo ship about to load a consignment of wood.

operations were moved a mile downriver to Friarton, where there was deeper water and space for industrial development close to the new railway line. Recently, the harbour's facilities and accessibility has been improved by dredging the river, replacing the navigation buoys and providing a harbour tender. The river from Dundee now features on the appropriate Admiralty charts, and can accommodate ships of 90 metres in length. As a result it continues to be an important commercial asset to the area, even though its financial viability suffers from a continuing dispute with Dundee, which levies charges on all ships passing through its waters, whether they dock at Dundee or not.

Extract from General Roy's
Military Map of Scotland

# Perth's Western Sector

As late as 1747 in Roy's military
map, there is no indication of any
road leading westwards from Perth
towards Stirling and Glasgow. It
seems that travellers and certainly
military baggage trains heading west
set out either by the Edinburgh Road
to Bridge of Earn, or by the Crieff
Road. And yet in mediaeval times the
kings of Scotland had a palace in
Forteviot, and must have travelled to
it regularly from Perth. Furthermore,
the strategic position of Pitheavlis
Castle, built 200 years before Roy's
survey, suggests that its purpose was
to monitor an important route from
the south-west into Perth.

## Needless Road, Necessity Brae
## and the Glasgow Road

Needless Road and Necessity Brae,
whether on Roy's map or not, were
for centuries one continuous track
heading south-west out of Perth
towards Forteviot. From the gates of
Perth at the South Port it was a long,
straight, steady climb of over three
miles to the ridge between the hills
overlooking Strathearn. It was
interrupted at roughly the halfway
point by the agricultural settlement
of Cherrybank, clustered round the
Cherrybank Inn. Here, where
Needless Road becomes Necessity
Brae and the incline steepens, men
and horses could take a break, and
quench their thirst.

The name 'Needless' derives from
the Scots words 'Neat' meaning
cattle, and 'Lea' or 'Leas' meaning a
meadow. Both words were
commonly used in the mid-18th
century by Robert Burns and others.

just north of the station, for what is now the Glasgow Road. This is the busiest route into Perth, bringing travellers to the city from the whole of central and west central Scotland and beyond. As the Glasgow Road winds up the hill, roughly parallel to the more direct line of Needless Road and Necessity Brae, it also touches the Cherrybank Inn, so that men and animals could still be refreshed, before taking a different route over the ridge to Strathearn.

Sadly, the continuity of Needless Road and Necessity Brae was broken by housing developments in the late 19th century, and it is now necessary to divert from the top of Needless Road onto the Glasgow Road, and go round the Cherrybank Inn in order to rejoin the old route to the west.

## Pitheavlis Castle

This A-listed castle sits at a strategic point on Needless Road, from whence it dominated the western access to Perth. Built in the late 16th century, it is an L-shaped laird's tower house, complete with crow stepped gables and pepper pot turrets with conical roofs. In the 19th century a large extension was built on its north side. The interior of the castle is now divided into apartments, which command broad views across the rooftops of Perth.

The 'Neat Leas' Road provided access to the city and its markets for the cattle that were grazed on the slopes of Craigie Hill. Necessity Brae, on the other hand, derived its name from the necessity to hire extra horses at the Cherrybank Inn to pull heavy loads up the long steep hill.

However, in 1847 this route out of Perth was suddenly and completely blocked by the new railway station, and in due course Needless Road became no more than a suburban street with a long history. At the same time, a bridge was built

### A Ball for a Prince

In September 1745, when Prince Charles Edward Stewart occupied Perth on his way south to the Battle of Prestonpans, the ladies of Perth organised a ball in his honour in Pitheavlis castle.

## Aviva

In 1983 the General Accident Company (see Chapter 7) moved out of the city centre to new modern headquarters on the Pitheavlis Estate, off Necessity Brae. This innovative concrete building consists of tiered terraces, built into the north slope of Craigie Hill, with each terrace looking out onto a garden on the roof of the terrace below. The result is a huge office complex with an inconspicuous profile when approached from the city. Most of the offices are open plan, light and airy. The building was expensively fitted out and decorated, including much use of elm and rosewood. A ceramic *Name Wall* by Mike de Haan and a tapestry, *Hills of Perth*, by Samantha Ainsley in the marble entrance foyer received Saltire Society Arts and Crafts in Architecture Awards in 1983.

Rationalisation in the insurance industry dealt a death blow to the independence of the General Accident Company, which merged first with the Commercial Union and then the merged company joined the Norwich Union to become, eventually, Aviva. Nevertheless, Aviva have maintained a strong presence in Perth, which is one of its 'Centres of Excellence'.

### The Return of the Prodigal Statue by Ronald Rae

Looking down over Perth from the grassy slope beside the drive leading to the Aviva headquarters is the massive granite statue, *The Return of the Prodigal*, by Ronald Rae. It was commissioned by General Accident to interpret their motto, 'I warn and I protect', and given to Perth to celebrate the company's move to their new headquarters. Rae's inspiration came from Rembrandt's painting, *The Prodigal Son*, which is in The Hermitage in St Petersburg. In his interpretation, Rae depicts a defiant father clasping his delinquent son to his bosom.

Sculpture by Ronald Rae – *Return of the Prodigal*.

Dewars centre.
MAP 1 · C7

Perth leisure pool.
MAP 1 · D7

## Dewars Centre and the Perth Leisure Pool

These are separate but adjacent facilities built in 1988–90 on the site of Dewars offices and bonded warehouse (see Chapter 5). The complex consists of an exhibition and conference centre with a large curling rink, an indoor bowling arena, and, in a separate building, an award winning swimming pool and leisure centre. The Dewars Centre regularly hosts the Scottish International Open for bowls, and the British Isles Indoor Bowls

An old curling stone that might have been used in many village matches.

A match between Canada and Scotland at the ice rink in Dewars Centre.

© Live Active Leisure, Perth.

Championship. However, it is the curling rink that brings most international competitors to Perth.

## Curling in Perth

Perth is proud of its curling heritage and of the current prominence of Perthshire curlers in the international game. As St Andrews is the home of golf, so Perth in Scotland is the home of curling. From mediaeval times, the sport was played in northern Europe, including Scotland, and indeed the earliest written record of curling

comes from the records of Paisley Abbey in 1541, while the earliest continental records are two paintings by the Dutch master Pieter Bruegel, dated 1565. Even older is the oldest curling stone in the world, engraved with the date 1511, which was found at the bottom of the Lake of Menteith in the historic County of Perthshire. The inscription is probably not contemporaneous with the stone, but there is no doubt that it is an excellent example of the earliest form of curling stone and could well have been used in the 16th century. In 1975, local government boundary changes moved West Perthshire into the Stirling District, and the stone is now exhibited in the Stirling Museum. Nevertheless, a large number of old curling stones are exhibited in Dewar's Centre, and there are other old stones which are ornaments in suburban gardens.

Although the game was mostly played in rural areas, the rules were codified in Edinburgh by the Grand Caledonian Curling Club in 1838. However, Perth played an important role in that club's development. In 1842, during the visit of Queen Victoria and Prince Albert to Perth, the Queen expressed an interest in the game, and so the Earl of Mansfield demonstrated the technique by 'throwing' a curling stone down the polished floor of the Long Gallery of Scone Palace. The Queen was so impressed that she authorised an immediate change in the club's name to the Royal Caledonian Curling Club, and Prince Albert became its first president!

Perth is still important in world

curling. In 1965, six curling nations met in Perth – Canada, Norway, Sweden, Switzerland, the USA and, of course, Scotland. At that meeting the International Curling Federation (ICF) was set up, and a successful campaign started to have curling recognised as an Olympic sport. In 1991 the ICF changed its name to the World Curling Federation, which is now the world governing body of the Olympic winter sport of curling and the Paralympic sport of wheelchair curling. It has a permanent secretariat of 15, which is based at its head-quarters in 74 Tay Street, Perth.

The rink at Dewars Centre has eight sheets, and is renowned for the quality of its ice. It regularly hosts large international matches, among which is the Perth Mercure Masters championship, which brings 16 international teams to Perth in the first week of January, to play 16 Scottish teams in a knockout competition.

JEANFIELD ROAD

ordered symmetry of these buildings provides a glimpse of a less hectic past, peopled by disciplined nurses and autocratic sisters wearing starched headdresses.

## Perth Royal Infirmary

Opened in 1914 by King George V, Perth Royal Infirmary (PRI) assumed the care of Perth's sick and infirm from the old City and County Infirmary (now the AK Bell Library). The main entrance is now from Jeanfield Road, and it leads to a typically chaotic modern hospital site, smothered in roads and car parks, and littered with box-like modern buildings. However, it is still possible to have an unrestricted view of the original two-storey Neo-Georgian ward blocks, each with balconies and square corner towers, topped by elaborate cupolas. The

## The Famous Grouse

Perth's newest, and largest, item of public art is the huge statue of a grouse taking flight as if from a heather moor. The statue is situated above the Broxden roundabout on Perth's south-western bypass and looks down on traffic to and from Glasgow, Edinburgh, Inverness, Aberdeen and Dundee. Because of the scale of the statue, the tops of the conifer trees on the roundabout appear like the heather on a moor.

The statue was commissioned by Edrington Distillers, the makers of the Famous Grouse blend of Scotch whisky (see Chapter 5), and was the

Original wards in Perth Royal Infirmary.
MAP 2 · E3

Jeanfield Road, a corruption of the original name 'Gin Field Road'.

**PERTH ROYAL INFIRMARY University Teaching Hospital** is the proud notice at the main entrance of PRI, and indeed that is now the case. However, back in 2003 it seemed that a 'death from 1,000 cuts' was about to be inflicted on PRI, and across Perthshire there was a crisis of confidence in the NHS. As well as cost cutting, PRI was experiencing difficulties in recruiting able, ambitious, middle grade staff who provide the backbone of clinical services. Increasingly, young doctors were avoiding hospitals like PRI for the career enhancing opportunities of work in a teaching hospital. The solution was to amalgamate PRI with Dundee's Ninewells Hospital and the Medical School of Dundee University, unite the various medical, surgical and other units in the two hospitals, and rotate the staff between them. So now consultants and their teams, professors, clinical lecturers, medical scientists and nurses work across both hospitals. They see patients in clinics and ward rounds, teach medical students, and carry out operations, and undertake research on both sites.

As well as improving the quality and accessibility of care for the people of Perthshire, the change has relieved pressure on Ninewells Hospital in Dundee, broadened its clinical resource base, and provided a flexibility that did not exist before.

Perth Royal Infirmary, Hospital.

company's contribution to the commemoration of Perth's 800th anniversary in 2010. The artist, Ruaraig Maciver, built it by bending and welding steel rods into shape. It was then galvanised, giving it a light grey appearance which shimmers in the sunlight, and when floodlit. It is a very worthy addition to Perth's public art.

# North-west and North

Perth's northern suburbs cover a wedge of urban territory extending from Atholl Street to the River Almond, and straddling the Dunkeld and Crieff Roads and the Perth Lade. There are a number of important civic, retail and industrial buildings, but the area consists mostly of a mixture of 20th century commercial and housing developments, the latter including the North Muirton scheme, which was devastated by the floods of 1993.

## Police Station

At the apex of this wedge, occupying a prominent position adjacent to the Inner ring road is the HQ of Police Scotland's Perth & Kinross Division.

The Famous Grouse statue above the Broxden Roundabout at sunset.
© Edrington Distillers.
MAP 2 · C2

Built in 1977 as the command centre for the Western Division of Tayside Police, it is proof that Perth was not immune from the brutalist postmodern architecture of the 1970s.

## Highland House

At the southern edge of St Catherine's Retail Park is Highland House. This stylish building has had a chequered career. Built in 1885 as a dye works, it suffered a serious fire and was rebuilt in 1919–21, but continued as a dye works. After more changes it became the headquarters of the 51st Highland Division in 1949, and thereby acquired its name. Further changes of use took place in the late 1970s and 1980s, until it was closed by another fire in 1995. In 2001 it reopened as an important element in St Catherine's Retail Park, with shops on the ground floor and offices above. It makes a fine contrast to the dreary sheds that occupy most of the park.

## Dunkeld Road

Dunkeld Road leads from Atholl Street north to Dunkeld, Pitlochry and Inverness. Important buildings on Dunkeld Road include the headquarters of Scottish and Southern Electricity, the World Headquarters of Stagecoach, a major office of the Royal Bank of Scotland and the Queen's Barracks. This last is the headquarters of the 51st Highland, 7th Battalion the Royal Regiment of Scotland (7 Scots), formerly the Black Watch. It is the Territorial Army's infantry battalion for the North of Scotland.

The northern part of Dunkeld Road is lined for much of its length by motor dealerships, earning it the title, 'Perth's Motor Mile'. It is said that ten per cent of all the new cars sold in Scotland come from dealerships on this road.

Perth's Police Station.
MAP 1 · H13

Highland House in St Catherine's Retail Park.
MAP 1 · F14

Dunkeld Road, the 'Motor Mile'.

George Duncan Athletics Arena from the air. Perth Grammar School is on the left.
MAP 2 · F5

St John's Academy and the North Inch Campus from the air.

schools, St John's Academy, opened in 2011. This and its primary section occupy the North Inch Campus, along with a large local library and the music and drama facilities for the whole of Perth and Kinross. Here there are rehearsal facilities, storage for musical instruments and a substantial auditorium, which is used by many local organisations.

## University of the Highlands and Islands (Perth College)

The Crieff Road branches off the Dunkeld Road, crosses the Lade and the Railway, and then climbs steadily out of Perth to the north-west. As it ascends the steepest part of the hill, the complex of buildings on the left hand side, largely obscured by apartments and trees, is the largest campus of the University of the Highlands and Islands. It is built on a sloping 30-acre site, facing east across Perth and the Tay to the Sidlaw Hills. The Brahan Building, a four-storey, red brick construction on the very top of the site is its main teaching and administrative centre.

**The University of the Highlands and Islands** is a federation of 13 colleges and research institutions stretching from Shetland to Perth, and from the Western Isles to Moray. While the administrative centre is in Inverness, Perth has the largest campus and most students, including the greatest number of overseas students. It also has some of the most high profile academics, including Nobel Peace laureate, Professor Martin Price, who holds the UNESCO Chair in Sustainable Mountain Development.

## George Duncan Athletics Arena and the North Inch Campus

Lying between the Dunkeld Road and the River Tay, on the edge of the North Inch and its golf course and adjacent to the Muirton housing scheme, is the George Duncan Athletics Arena and its running track. Opened in 2008, it filled an important gap in Perth's sporting facilities, and enables regional and national athletic competitions to be held in the city.

The arena lies between Perth Grammar School, which was originally located at Princes Street Corner, and one of Perth's newest

## Football in Perth – McDiarmid Park

Further out the Crieff Road on the very edge of the city, adjacent to the western bypass is McDiarmid Park, the home of Perth's Premier Division football club, St Johnstone. The club was set up in 1885 by a group of young men, members of a cricket club of the same name, who wanted something to do in the winter. Initially the club played on the North Inch, but in 1824 it moved to Muirton Park, a purpose-built stadium on the Dunkeld Road, which was to be its home for 65 years. The club's fortunes fluctuated during the Muirton years, and by the mid-1980s were very low. The football results were bad, attendances were very poor, the stadium was crumbling and debts were mounting.

However, a new chairman, Geoff Brown (a local builder and entrepreneur), was appointed and he has turned the Club around. Muirton Park was sold to become an ASDA superstore, and a local farmer, Bruce McDiarmid, donated the land on which the new stadium was built to accommodate 10,000 spectators. It

was opened in 1989, and was the first all-seated stadium in the UK. In addition, there was parking for 1,000 cars and 100 coaches, a synthetic playing surface adjacent to the stadium, and conference facilities within the main building.

St Johnstone has had a number of spells in the top flight of Scottish football. Most recently, after several years in the Scottish First Division, it was promoted to the Premier Division in 2009, just in time to celebrate the 800th anniversary of Perth's Royal Charter in 2010, and contribute to the successful campaign for the restoration of City Status in 2012. It has finished high enough in the Scottish League to qualify for European competition five times. The most recent occasion was 2014, when the club also achieved its greatest success so far, by winning the Scottish Cup.

The Brahan Building, Perth College, UHI.
MAP 2 · E4

Stadium at McDiarmid Park.
MAP 2 · D5

# CHAPTER SIXTEEN

# Sir Walter Scott and the Fair Maid of Perth

## The Fair Maid's Trail

Perth owes a tremendous debt to Sir Walter Scott. The publication of *The Fair Maid of Perth* in 1828 put Perth on the map like no other event in the last 200 years. Ever since then, the term 'The Fair City', which Scott used in his novel more than 300 times, has been synonymous with Perth. The Fair Maid's Trail is a walk around the locations in Perth related to the story and to Sir Walter Scott. It begins at the North Inch.

## The 'Battle of the Clans' on the North Inch

While Scott's novel is fiction, it is based on the historical event of the Battle of the Clans. Furthermore, to give authenticity to his descriptions of events, Scott uses recognisable locations such as the North Inch, the Fair Maid's House, Hal's (or Henry's) house on Mill Wynd and the streets of old Perth.

*Battle of the Clans*. Unknown artist of the Scottish School. *c*.1850.
© Perth Museum & Art Gallery, Perth & Kinross Council.

In 1396 King Robert III summoned the rival clans Quhele, or Kay, and Chattan to settle their long-standing feud in mortal combat between 30 picked men from each clan. The action, reminiscent of Roman gladiatorial combat, took place on the North Inch in front of the King and the citizens of Perth. Sir Walter Scott inserted a romantic theme, involving Catharine, the daughter of Simon Glover, a successful Perth merchant, and Henry Gow, or Hal o' the Wynd (Henry of Mill Wynd), an armourer and prominent local swordsman.

In the week leading up to the battle, the king's son, the Duke of Rothesay, with his Master of Horse, Sir John Ramorny, attempt to abduct Catharine from her father's house on the North Port - the Fair Maid's House. However, they are thwarted by the fortuitous intervention of Henry Gow, Catharine's favoured suitor, who hacks off the hand of Sir John Ramorny. Meanwhile, another rivalry for Catharine's affection develops between Henry and Conachar, who becomes the Chief of the Kay clan on the death of his father, just before the battle.

As the clans assemble, Clan Chattan is one man short. Henry volunteers to replace him, in order to seize the opportunity to confront Conachar. Towards the end of the bloody battle, the two come face to face. Conachar flees by swimming the Tay, and then, overcome with shame, commits suicide. Henry, weary of battle and bloodshed, sheaths his sword and vows that henceforth he will fight only in Scotland's service, and is accepted by Catharine.

The explorers' room in the Fair Maid's House.

## Fair Maid's House

From the North Inch, cross Charlotte Street and head along the North Port towards the Concert Hall, behind which, lies the Fair Maid's House (see Chapter 10). This house, although not built until nearly 100 years after the Battle of the Clans, is the building Scott used in his novel as the model for the home of Simon Glover and his fair daughter, Catharine. It features in some of the most dramatic scenes in the book, and is therefore very important for Perth. The house has been much altered, and has had a number of uses, but is now, with the next-door building, Lord John Murray's House, the headquarters of the Royal Scottish Geographical Society (RSGS).

## Hal o' the Wynd's House

From the Fair Maid's House, proceed along Mill Street, cross Methven Street into West Mill Street to reach the City Mills. Opposite the Lower City Mills on Mill Wynd is Hal O' the Wynd's house, the home of Henry Gow. The central gable of this much altered 18th-century building stands forward slightly and consists of exposed rubble, contrasting with the

Hal o' the Wynd's House.
MAP 1 · J10

harled wings on each side. A pend through the house leads to North Methven Street. This building, in the centre of what was a very congested area around the City Mills, was used by Scott in his descriptions of places and events in his novel.

## Sculpture – The Fair Maid

From Hal o' the Wynd's House follow Mill Wynd, the mediaeval route from the City Mills to the centre of Perth, via Old High Street

The President (Mayor) of Bydgoszcz, Perth's twin city in Poland, gives the *Fair Maid* a hug.
© Angus Findlay.

*Right:*
King Robert III on the left, Lord Provost Charteris, on the right.

to the High Street, and then to its junction with Kirkside. There a lifesize bronze by Graeme Ibbeson (1995) of the *Fair Maid of Perth* sits on a bench facing the Tay. She looks more like a respectable auntie than a young lady whose beauty stimulated murderous rivalries among her suitors. Her pose, sitting reading a book (Sir Walter Scott's novel?), is an open invitation to visiting tourists and dignitaries to sit down, put an arm round her, and smile for the camera.

## Stained Glass – Old Council Chambers

From the bronze of the *Fair Maid*, walk the short distance down the

Left to right:

The Fair Maid, in the centre, Simon Glover on the left and Hal o' the Wynd on the right.

Duke of Rothesay on the left and the Glee Maiden on the right.

Sir Walter Scott statue on the South Inch.
MAP 1 · K3

High Street to the Old Council Chambers at 3 High Street. Seek permission to enter to see the stained-glass windows, which depict the main characters of Scott's novel. The central window of three panels features the Fair Maid, along with her father Simon Glover and Henry Gow. On either side are windows, each of two panels. The east window depicts King Robert III, and Sir Patrick Charteris (Lord Provost of Perth in 1881), and the west window the Duke of Rothesay and the Glee Maiden.

## Statue of Sir Walter Scott

It is right and proper to pay homage to the author of the book that has been so important for Perth. The lifesize statue of Sir Walter Scott with his dog, Maida, stands on the edge of the South Inch, looking across Marshall Place to King Street. Sculpted in 1845 by the Cochrane Brothers, it was acquired by the Council when it bought Cochrane's yard in the mid 19th century, after the family emigrated to Canada. The Cochrane Brothers also sculpted the statue of Thomas Hay Marshall.

# CHAPTER SEVENTEEN

# Shopping in Perth

INDEPENDENT SPECIALIST and niche shops are the lifeblood of the retail economy in Perth's city centre, and Perth is proud of its reputation as one the best places in Scotland to browse for items of quality which are not generally available in the large stores. The range of such shops is truly astonishing. High fashion shops for ladies' clothes, shoes and hats are perhaps most noticeable, but there are many others selling gifts, kilts, jewellery, sports equipment, herbal remedies, interior design etc. The list is long and very varied. There is even a specialist shop that makes and sells bespoke sporrans. These shops are spread across the city centre, complementing the outlets of the major chain stores, most of which have branches in Perth.

However, it is not only the variety of outlets that makes Perth attractive, it is also because the area involved is so compact and easily accessible on foot. Furthermore, the bus and railway stations are nearby, and there are park and ride facilities and plenty of affordable car parks. The most important shopping areas are within the line of the mediaeval city wall, but especially between the High Street and South Street, and also in the adjoining streets and vennels. In recent years the shopping area has gradually extended, especially to Princes Street in the south, and west up York Place and the Old High Street.

Perth's independent retailers do not only cater for tourists or for shopping for luxuries or Christmas presents. The basic staples of life can still be bought in the city centre. Some of the best independent butchers in Scotland

Perth's café culture in full swing in St John's Place.
MAP 1 · P8

Jim Fairlie, one of the pioneers of Perth Farmers' Market.

are from Perthshire, and have outlets in the city centre, and there are innumerable bakers, and some very high-class delicatessens, shops for the immigrant Polish community, as well as the indispensible Marks & Spencer, Sainsbury's Local and Tesco Metro.

Almost as important as the shops is the astonishing number of cafés, pubs, tearooms and restaurants of every conceivable type. They vary from home-grown fine-dining establishments, serving the very best of Scottish produce, to transatlantic chains and restaurants specialising in food from the continent and farther afield. The various quality marks that protect the reputation of locally sourced Scottish meat and seafood are much in evidence, and most of the restaurants and many of the hotels are members of Cittaslow (see Chapter 19). This trend to the service sector has, in Perth, taken the sting out of the decline in shopping as the internet and out of town shopping malls has drained the retail market from the town centres of Scotland. The percentage of empty retail property in Perth city centre is the lowest of all the cities and major towns in Scotland.

As part of its drive to look outwards to Europe, Perth has made a conscious effort to develop an outdoor café culture, with tables and chairs, colourful canopies and umbrellas and flowers spilling out onto the wide pavements. Several very successful French restaurants are now well integrated into the commercial life of the city, and Perth's long standing Chinese community plays an active role in

Many of Perth's retailers decorate their shop fronts with hanging baskets purchased from the Council's nurseries.

this area. There are also Italian, Polish and Mexican establishments, as well as the usual fish and chip shops and Indian takeaways. Furthermore, most of the big stores have in-house cafés, some of them new, and others with a pedigree extending back many decades.

In Perth it is never difficult to take a rest from the foot slogging of retail therapy, or to enjoy a break from debates at a conference, and wind down and relax in very agreeable surroundings.

## Three Centuries of Retailing

The shopping experience in modern Perth encapsulates elements from half a millennium of retailing. The monthly Farmers' Market on Saturdays differs little from its mediaeval predecessors, apart from its standards of cleanliness and the availability of refrigerators. It was established in 1999 by Perth &

Kinross Council and a group of local farmers, and was the first such market in Scotland. It is now a farmers' co-operative and has been the source of a number of successful 'spin-out' farming and food businesses across Perthshire. Its success was recognised by Prince Charles, Duke of Rothesay who requested a special weekday Farmers' Market to coincide with his visit to Perth to celebrate the 800th anniversary of the King William Charter.

The stalls and equipment used for the Farmers' Market are made

available to other markets – in particular the ancient traditional Andermass Market at the end of November, and at the Christmas Market. More modern developments are the continental markets, which are held in the spring and summer, and the Art Market on Tay Street, which is part of the Perth Festival of the Arts. Usually on market days the Perth & District Pipe band, or Perthshire Brass, the local brass band provides musical entertainment.

While Perth's outdoor markets are the modern equivalents of mediaeval shopping, scattered throughout the city are persisting examples of retail architecture spanning the last 250

Late 18th-century shop architecture in George Street.

Take-away. Victorian shop architecture, but put to a modern use.

Kilt shop in Methven Street. Its deep arcaded entrance, allows a maximum of natural light into the shop.

**Safer Shopping and Best Bar None Awards**

Perth & Kinross Council, the local shops, pubs and cafés, the police and many voluntary and statutory bodies have worked together to safeguard Perth's shoppers. As a result, Perth is the only place in Scotland to win the Safer Shopping Award three times since it was instituted in 2006. Furthermore, in relation to the night-time economy, more than half of the licensed premises in Perth have won awards in the Best Bar None scheme, which seeks to develop high standards in the licensed trade.

years. Look out for AS Deuchar's antiques shop at 12 South Street, a genuine survivor from the late 18th century with its small panes of ripple glass, and in Scott Street, Methven Street and George Street note the examples from the end of the 19th and early 20th century with their large windows and cast iron supports to admit the maximum amount of light. Mid and late 20th-century shops are well represented in central Perth, and there is also the covered arcade of the St John's Centre.

St Catherine's Retail Park completes the shopping mix for Perth city. Unlike most such parks it is within reasonable walking distance of the city centre, being located adjacent to the Inner Ring Road near its junction with the Dunkeld Road.

*Clockwise:*
Prince Charles visits the Farmers' Market .
© Angus Findlay.

Perthshire Brass providing entertainment at the Farmers' Market, in front of the City Hall.

Andermass Fair on a cold November day.
© Perth & Kinross Council.

Continental Market.
© Perth & Kinross Council.

# CHAPTER EIGHTEEN

# Perth's War Memorials

LIKE TOWNS AND cities across Scotland, Perth has many war memorials, including some iconic and very unusual ones. And yet it does not have an outside memorial that on Remembrance Day can be the focus of the city's homage to those who paid the ultimate sacrifice. There is nowhere for military and civic dignitaries to lay wreaths, and no saluting base past which the armed services can parade. Perth's memorial is inside St John's Kirk, and generally available only in the context of a church service. And so the Edward VII memorial, outside the St John's Centre in King Edward Street, is regularly pressed into service as a substitute.

## Perth's War Memorial in St John's Kirk

The restoration of St John's Kirk after the First World War was considered to be Perth's memorial to the fallen of the War. Within the Kirk, however, the official War Memorial is the shrine, which occupies what was a small chapel on the west side of the north transept of the Kirk. Designed by Sir Robert Lorimer, it is in the form of an altar within a gothic arch. At the pinnacle of the arch is the Royal Coat of Arms of Scotland, and beneath it two angels hold a crown and Saltire above a frame containing the text of the memorial.

TO THE GLORY OF GOD
AND IN GRATEFUL MEMORY
OF THOSE OF THE
COUNTY AND CITY OF PERTH
WHO FELL IN
THE GREAT WAR 1914–1919
WHOSE NAMES ARE WRITTEN
IN THE GOLDEN BOOK
WITHIN THE SHRINE
THIS CHURCH OF
JOHN THE BAPTIST
WAS RESTORED
1923 – 26
GREATER LOVE
HATH NO MAN THAN THIS
THAT A MAN LAY DOWN HIS LIFE
FOR HIS FRIENDS

Columns on either side carry a list of the main theatres of battle, including 'in the air', and 'on the sea'. On the altar are laid two 'Golden Books' containing the names of those who perished in each of the World Wars.

At the sides of the shrine are two angels carrying shields: one depicting the Lamb of St John, and the other the Lion Rampant of Scotland. On the south side of the chapel is the Colour of the Perth Branch of the Burma Star Association, which was laid up in 1996. On the other side a wooden plaque carrying 16 names of the 'Men of St John's Kirk' who died in the 1939–45 war. Standing by the

entrance to the shrine is a statue of John the Baptist by the Indian sculptor Fanindra Bose.

The shrine is lit by a three light window by Morris Meredith Williams. It depicts the Archangel Michael, clad in armour and brandishing a sword. On either side are two bands of warrior angels with spears carrying banners proclaiming Courage, Faith, Fortitude, Hope, Magnanimity and Endurance, with which they are destroying the many-headed dragon of greed, torment and cruelty.

The shrine is one of Lorimer's finest works. On Remembrance Sunday, it is the focus of a major parade, including all the armed services, the Lord Lieutenant of Perth & Kinross, the Provost, councillors and senior officials, escorted by the Society of High Constables.

## Other Memorials in St John's Kirk

There are two other plaques in the vicinity of the shrine: a bronze dedicated to the men from Perthshire who lost their lives in the Parachute Regiment and the British Airborne Special Forces and a brass plaque celebrating the war effort of the Women's Royal Army Corps. On a nearby pillar hangs a very colourful tapestry depicting the many aspects of the life of the 51st Highland Division.

On the east wall of the south aisle of St John's Kirk there is a further

The shrine.

The shrine window, St John's Kirk.

Statue of John the Baptist by Fanindra Bose.

memorial commemorating the
gallantry of the officers and men of
'HM 90th Light Infantry, Perthshire
Volunteers', who fell in the Crimean
War, 1854–55. In the south wall of the
Choir, a window commemorates the
28 members of the East Church
congregation who gave their lives in
the First World War.

## Perth's Memorial Garden

Perth's memorial garden has been
established in the small amphitheatre
enclosed by the flood defence scheme
and some trees, at the entrance to the
North Inch. Here are a number of
memorials, and in the future, any
new ones will be located on this site.

### 51st Highland Division
### Memorial

The most important of these is Alan
Herriot's bronze statue of a Dutch
girl presenting a rose to a kilted
Highland soldier. Symbolically, he is

carrying his bagpipes and not a gun.
Two casts were made from the same
mould to commemorate the advance
of the 51st Highland Division across
Europe in 1944. One was unveiled
on 23 October 1994, in the Dutch
town of Schijndel to commemorate
the 50th anniversary of the liberation
of the town by the Highland Division
in 1944. Perth's statue was unveiled
on 13 May 1995 on the 50th
anniversary of VE Day.

The statue stands on a plinth, the
long sides of which feature bronze
reliefs of battlefield scenes. One of
the short sides lists the Division's
Regimental Battle Honours and the
other is a tribute to the men who
served.

There are two matching granite
columns adjacent to the monument.
One features a poem, 'Tunes and
Flowers', by Andrew McGeaver, the
words of which have been cut into
the face of the column.

On the face of the second column

is a brass plaque, which was presented to the Provost of Perth by the people of the village of Gennep in the Netherlands, on the occasion of the final reunion of the members of the 51st Highland Division Veteran's Association on 8 June 2008. Gennep is the village on the banks of the River Maas, part of the Rhine delta, from which the 51st Division launched the offensive to cross the Rhine into Germany. The battle lasted from the 9th to the 14th of February 1945, and completely destroyed the village.

At the top of the plaque is 'HD', the emblem of the Highland Division (disparagingly, but jealously, referred to as the Highland Decorators by other regiments), and the heading in English and Dutch, 'IN REMEMBRANCE OF OUR LIBERATORS'. The plaque is inscribed with the name of each of the 46 soldiers who died, the crests of the units in which they served, and the date of death. There were 19 men from the Black Watch, 17 from the Gordon Highlanders, four from the Derbyshire Yeomanry, three Royal Engineers, two from the Royal Artillery and one from the King's Own Royal Borders Regiment.

*Clockwise:*

51st Highland Division Regimental Battle Honours.

Bronze plaque below the 51st Highland Division Memorial.

Gennep plaque.

'Tunes and Flowers', poem by Andrew McGreaver.

Memorial to the Perthshire
members of the International
Brigades in the Spanish Civil
War.

Lynedoch Monument.
MAP 1 · P13

Bowerswell House.
MAP 1 · V11

## Other Memorials

There are two further memorials on the floodwall, on either side of the floodgates. One is for the men and women of Perthshire who fought in the International Brigades against fascism in Spain between 1936 and 1939. On it is inscribed a verse from a poem by William Soutar:

> *Even as blossoms fall*
> *Circling about a tree*
> *Our deeds within a world*
> *Define our world.*

The second one is a plaque, rescued from a disused building which commemorates the employees of the Perth Co-operative Society Ltd who were killed in the two world wars.

## Lynedoch Monument

Nearby is the Lynedoch Monument, a large obelisk of polished grey granite, the work of local craftsmen David Beveridge & Sons. It is not strictly a war memorial, being erected in 1896 to commemorate the raising of the 90th Regiment of Foot (Perthshire Volunteers), by Thomas Graham, later Baron Lynedoch. The Volunteers saw much distinguished service, notably in the Crimea (see memorial in St John's Kirk), before being incorporated into the Cameronians in 1881, and disbanded in 1968.

## Bowerswell

In 1946, when other towns and cities were adding panels to existing First World War memorials, Perth decided to have a 'living memorial'. Bowerswell House, the beautiful Italianate villa on the east bank of the river, and the home of the Gray family (see Chapter 13) came on the market. A public subscription was launched, and the house and grounds were purchased for £5,000. The house was converted into a retirement home with 21 apartments, and a further 22 semi-detached cottages were built in the grounds. The two main rooms of the house, with their elaborate plaster ceilings, were retained unaltered to be used as common rooms by the residents. The original purpose was to provide good quality accommodation for ex-servicemen.

There is another Golden Book containing the names of those who died and a small conventional war memorial in the grounds, which was

## Thomas Graham, Baron Lynedoch

Graham was a remarkable man. Born in 1748, the first half of his life was spent managing his several Perthshire estates, including Lyndoch, just west of Perth, where he lived with his wife, the Honourable Mary Cathcart. She was an exquisite society beauty and was painted by Gainsborough, when he was at the peak of his ability as a portrait painter. The painting, *The Honourable Mrs Graham*, is now one of the best known of all 18th century portraits. Her health, however, was poor, and she died of tuberculosis aged only 35. Following her death, her grief stricken husband put the painting into storage, where it languished for 40 years until after his death. His heirs bequeathed the painting to the National Gallery of Scotland, on the condition that it should never leave Edinburgh. It is now one of the gallery's most prized exhibits.

Meanwhile, Graham, at the age of 45, decided that on account of 'intolerable loneliness' he would enter military life. He proved to be an able battle strategist and a courageous and inspiring leader, able to turn desperate situations into victories. One such was the Battle of Barossa in 1811, which turned the tide of the Peninsular War against Napoleon, leading eventually to the victory at Waterloo. Eventually Graham became Wellington's second in command, although 20 years his senior. He was created Baron Lynedoch in 1814, and in 1815 he received the Freedom of Perth. His full-length portrait hangs in the Perth Museum and Art Gallery.

He died in London in 1843, aged 96. His body was shipped to Dundee, and then transported by carriage to Methven, where he was buried in the family mausoleum. As his coffin passed through Perth, a muffled bell at St John's Kirk tolled a salute, and two cannons, mounted on the ramparts of Bellwood Mansion, above Riverside Park, were fired. The cannons are now in Perth Museum.

Portrait of Baron Lynedoch, by Sir John Lawrence. © Perth Museum & Art Gallery, Perth & Kinross Council.

# War Memorials Elsewhere in Perth

## Polish War Memorial

Following the fall of France in 1940, the Polish army was reformed in Scotland, and continued the fight as part of the Allied forces. After the War, with Poland under Russian domination, many Polish servicemen chose to remain in Scotland. In Perth a number of organisations kept the Polish culture alive and maintained links with the homeland.

In a section of Wellshill Cemetery, off Jeanfield Road, there are over 300 graves of Polish ex-servicemen behind the striking Polish War Memorial. Under the Eagle of Poland is the legend in English and Polish:

ETERNAL GLORY

TO THE POLISH SODIERS

WHO DIED IN 1939–45

FOR YOUR FREEDOM AND OURS

Each year, on the Sunday preceding Remembrance Sunday, a memorial service is conducted at the cemetery attended by the Polish Consul General for Scotland, along with civic and parliamentary representatives, and many Polish exiles. It is followed by Mass said in Polish in the Roman Catholic Church of St John the Baptist in Melville Street.

One of the Bowerswell semi-detached cottages.

Bowerswell War Memorial.

Polish War Memorial and grave stones.
MAP 1 · A12

unveiled on the 50th anniversary of VE day in 1995. In 2011 the management of the Bowerswell was taken over by a local Housing Association, and the Golden Book has been relocated to the AK Bell Library, where it can be viewed by interested individuals.

On Remembrance Day, the 11th of November, there is a service held in Bowerswell House, taken by the minister of Kinnoull Church, and attended by the Provost of Perth. The silence for two minutes is observed and then wreathes are laid at the memorial.

## North Korean War Memorial Garden

Perth's least known war memorial commemorates the 1,087 British servicemen killed in the Korean War. The garden is said to be a 'Korean Pagoda Garden'. The memorial consists of a section of wall painted with the outline map of South Korea, the insignia of the United Nations and that of the Commonwealth, the Korean badge, and the flags of the nations that took part in the conflict. A plaque records that it was installed by the Korean Veterans' Association, No. 1 Branch, Perth, to commemorate those killed in Korea from 1950 to 1953. It was opened officially in 2005.

This memorial is to be found in Lindsay Court, through a pend at 250 Old High Street.

## The Jeanfield and District Lads, and Other Memorials

This stone and marble monument to 67 Jeanfield and District Lads who were killed in the First World War is located in a corner of Wellshill cemetery at the end of Hawarden Terrace, off Jeanfield Road. There are numerous other memorials inside churches, inside the Masonic Lodge, on the wall of Pullar House, and adjacent to the entrance to the Aviva building.

Korean War Memorial Garden.
MAP 1 · J9

BKVA (British Korean Veteran's Association) chair in the Korean War Memorial Garden.

Jeanfield and District Memorial to 'Oor Ain Lads'.
MAP 2 · E3

# CHAPTER NINETEEN

# Civic Perth

## Past, Present and Future

Perth's history as the first capital, and subsequently the second city of Scotland, has resulted in a legacy of civic organisations and traditions, some of which have left their marks on the city's built fabric, and others on the programme of events that takes place regularly throughout the year. Its ambition to be counted as small but successful European city has expressed itself in the 'Bloom' competitions, in membership of the Cittaslow organisation, and more recently in its pursuit of the Europe Prize.

The Provost's badge and double chain.

The Lady Provost's badge and chain.

### Perth & Kinross Council

Civic authority in Perth is vested in Perth & Kinross Council, which was created by the reorganisation of Local Government in 1996, and which is responsible for an area of over 2,000 square miles and a population of 147,000. Of these, approximately 45,000 live in the City of Perth. The Council has 41 councillors, of whom 12 are elected from three multi-member wards which cover the city. Historically the present Council, and its predecessors have valued tradition, and continue to promote ceremonies such as the annual Kirking of the Council.

During the Victorian era Scotland's Town and City Councils, with the exception of Perth, all produced elaborate chains of office, with showy badges often studded with precious and semi-precious stones. These were designed to project the importance of the city or town on occasions such as royal visits, and important gatherings in Edinburgh.

However, Perth's Provost's badge and double chain of office date from the previous century and are among Scotland's oldest civic emblems to be worn regularly on public occasions. Their provenance is impeccable. The handwritten Council Minutes of March 1791 authorising the expenditure on badges and chains for the Provost and Bailies, record that, '... it being particularly necessary when they (the magistrates) are called upon to quell mobs or tumults that they should have some marks to distinguish them from the other inhabitants'. Later in 1791, there is an entry in the city ledger: 'To James Cornfute Goldsmith, for gold chain and medal for the Provost, and gold chains to the Dean of Guild, four Baillies and Convener: £180.'

In Perth a male provost's wife has the courtesy position and title of Lady Provost and a rather beautiful badge to go with it. This came about because in 1950 the ladies of Perth felt that Lady Ure-Primrose, the wife of Sir John Ure-Primrose, the Lord Provost at the time, should also have a badge of office. The various guilds and ladies' organisations came together and raised the money and commissioned an appropriate badge from Cairncross, jewellers in St John Street. The badge consists of the coat of arms of the City and Royal Burgh of Perth, and 'Lady Provost' inscribed on a scroll. It can be worn as a brooch or hanging below a Saltire on a silver chain of thistle emblems, interspersed with amethysts.

## Guildry Incorporation of Perth

The King William the Lion Charter of 1210, which confirmed Perth's status as a Royal Burgh, also established the 'Merchant Gild' to regulate trade in the burgh, by granting monopolies to 'merchant

burgesses'. In return, the merchants paid taxes to the king. In due course the Merchant Gild became the Guildry Incorporation, which was the predecessor of the Burgh Council, although the change to elected status happened slowly and in stages. This link is perpetuated by the traditional inclusion of the Lord Dean of Guild, in full ceremonial dress at all of Perth's ceremonial parades and church services.

There were eight trades represented in the Guildry – Baxters (bakers), Cordiners (shoemakers), Fleshers (butchers), Glovers, Hammermen, Tailors, Weavers and Wrights – and they have all left their marks on the streets and buildings of Perth. While each guild had its own premises (the Glovers, for example in the Fair Maid's House, the Wrights in the Watergate, and the Fleshers in South Street), the Incorporation's prestigious headquarters was the Guildhall on the High Street (see Chapter 7). However, its affairs are now run from an office in George Street. The Guildry has always been deeply involved in civic occasions. A pillar in the Tay Street floodwall records the event in 1633 when the Glovers' Incorporation performed a sword dance for Charles I when he was in Perth for his coronation. The text inscribed on the stone is:

Charles I was crowned in Scotland in 1633. He visited Perth and near this spot was entertained by a dance. Members of the Glovers' Incorporation of Perth performed a sword dance on a wooden stage moored on the River.

Among the earliest surviving
records of Guild proceedings in
Scotland is Perth's 'Lockit Book', a
leather-bound volume with two iron
clasps and locks, containing the
records of the organisation from
1452. In it are the signatures of
James VI in 1601, Charles II in 1650,
Queen Victoria in 1842, and more
recently, Prince Charles in 1995, and
HM the Queen in 2012. Interestingly,
Charles II's signature and defiant
phrase, '*Nemo me impune lacessit*' is
dated 24 July 1650, nearly six months
before his actual coronation as King
of Scots at Scone on 1 January 1651,
and ten years before his coronation

in London in 1660. The Lockit Book
is kept in a carved wooden box,
made from a rafter taken from the
Fair Maid's House.

The right to Guildry membership
is passed from father to son, although
new members can 'buy in' to the
organisation. Current membership of
the Guildry is therefore worldwide,
and many attend the triennial
meetings of the Incorporation from
afar. Daughters may not be members
but can transmit the right to their
husbands or sons. In modern times
the purpose of the Guildry has
become entirely charitable, and it
raises and distributes substantial
sums each year. Much of the income
comes from rents from its farming
and other property in and around the
appropriately named village of
Guildtown to the north of Perth.

Ten Scottish towns and cities, and
Berwick-upon-Tweed, have surviving
Guildries that are members of the
Court of the Deans of Guild of
Scotland. Of these Perth's Guildry is
the longest established. Perth's Lord
Dean survived the demotion inflicted
upon the Lord Provostship of Perth
in 1975, probably because the
zealous reformers undertaking the
reorganisation of local government
were unaware of the title.

## The Society of High Constables of the City of Perth

Law and order in mediaeval Scottish
burghs was maintained by 'Constables'
appointed by the burgh magistrates.
This was confirmed by James VI in an
Act of Parliament in 1617, and
continued for over 200 years. Then,

following the establishment of London's Metropolitan Police in 1829, paid police forces were set up across Scotland, under the supervision of a superintendent, and the former constables became, in effect, redundant. In Perth, however, they 'became re-nominated' (to quote from the history of the Society) as Members of the Society of High Constables of the City of Perth, and their chief officer became the Moderator of the Society. A similar process took place in the old Royal Burgh of Edinburgh, and in the Burghs of Leith and Holyrood. Perth's Society is therefore one of only four in Scotland.

The full complement of the Perth Society is 100 High Constables. Membership, which is by invitation from the governing Council, is limited to men living or working in

Perth. New members take an Oath of Allegiance, which must be witnessed by the Provost of Perth, even though the Provost will usually not be a member of the Society. The High Constables' duties are entirely ceremonial, the most important being to form a guard of honour for the Provost and councillors when on civic parades, when they march under the orders of the most senior Police officer in Perth.

## Civic Parades

Each year Perth & Kinross Council stages a number of important civic parades which blend tradition with modern relevance, and bring together different elements of Perth society. These parades are led by the Perth and District Pipe Band, which was founded in 1893. The band's Pipe Major is Perth's official City Piper, and he carries a banner attached from the base drone of his pipes with the Perth & Kinross Council coat of arms on one side, and the band's coat of

The Moderator of the Society of High Constables, with his top hat and ceremonial truncheon.
Courtesy of Tom Morrison.

A civic parade passes along King Edward Street, escorted by the High Constables.
© Perth & Kinross Council.

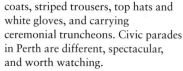

coats, striped trousers, top hats and
white gloves, and carrying
ceremonial truncheons. Civic parades
in Perth are different, spectacular,
and worth watching.

Most civic parades end in St
John's Kirk, where the Provost,
Councillors and Council officers file
into the council pews in the south
transept of the Kirk, behind the coat
of arms of the old Royal Burgh of
Perth. The High Constables sit in the
Guildry pews opposite, in the north
transept, behind the coat of arms of
the Perth & Kinross District Council.

arms, which is identical to the coat
of arms of the old City and Royal
Burgh of Perth on the other.

In these parades the Provost, the
Deputy Provost, and Lord Dean of
Guild all wear ermine trimmed red
robes, bicorn hats and their badges
and chains of office, and are
accompanied by the Lord Lieutenant
of Perth and Kinross, other
Councillors, magistrates and senior
Council officers. They are flanked on
either side by a full complement of
High Constables, dressed in morning

**Kirking of the Council** Every year the
elected members and senior officers
of the Council, flanked by the High
Constables, and preceded by the
Perth and District Pipe Band parade
to the High Kirk of St John for the
annual service of Kirking, or
rededication, at the beginning of the
Council's administrative year in May.
The event takes place on a Sunday
morning in late May, and is
particularly significant in those years
when it follows immediately after a
Council election.

**Remembrance Day Parade** On
Remembrance Sunday there are
coordinated, but separate, military
and civic parades to St John's Kirk
for the service of Remembrance
during which the two minutes
silenced is observed, and wreathes
are laid at the shrine inside the
church. After the service the civic
parade, led by the Perth and District
band leaves the Kirk first, and
marches to the promontory on Tay
Street where it is dismissed. The

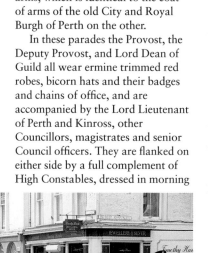

Provost, the Lord Lieutenant, and senior military officers then take up positions on a dais erected on the promontory, to await the military parade and take the salute. The military parade generally consists of one or two bands, a detachment of soldiers, and a large number of veterans and cadets from the three services.

**Other Parades** While the Kirking and Remembrance Day parades are held every year on specific days, there are other parades, which happen irregularly. Whenever the Third Battalion of the Royal Regiment of Scotland, formerly the Black Watch, returns from a tour of duty abroad, there is a Homecoming Parade, followed by a reception. Both the Third Battalion and the Seventh (Territorial) Battalion of the Royal Regiment have been presented with the Freedom of Perth, and therefore march through Perth, 'with bayonets fixed, drums beating, and colours flying', as is their right. It all makes for a fine spectacle. On important civic occasions, such as the 800th

Herr Elsaesser, Burgermeister of Aschaffenburg reads a lesson during the church service.
© Perth & Kinross Council.

Veterans enjoy soaking up the atmosphere of a military parade.
© Perth Picture Agency.

Soldiers of the Black Watch pass the saluting base at a Homecoming parade.
© Angus Findlay Photography.

Canadians from Perth's twin city in Ontario provide an informal element to the parade.
© Perth & Kinross Council.

Perth, the flowering city.
© Angus Findlay Photography.

Thistle flowerbed, Charlotte Street.

Award winning 'Bloom' display.

Cittaslow logo. A town on the back of a snail.
© Cittaslow.

anniversary of Perth's Royal Charter, representatives of our twin cities are invited to take part in the parade and the celebrations.

## Perth in Bloom

Ever since the publication of Sir Walter Scott's *Fair Maid of Perth* in 1828, Perth has claimed the title, 'The Fair City'. Over the last 30 years there has been a continuous

campaign to promote the 'Fair' image, especially through the 'Bloom' competitions, not only in Perth itself but across the whole Council area. This has been so successful that now among the cognoscenti of municipal flower power, Perth is a byword for success across the UK. Perth itself, and towns and villages from across Perth & Kinross, have regularly triumphed in the 'Beautiful Scotland' and 'Beautiful Britain' competitions, and starred in Europe and North America as well.

## Cittaslow

In 2003 Perth was looking for a way to build on its 'Fair City' reputation and promote itself as a food town at the centre of a large agricultural hinterland producing top quality food and drink. The Council also wished to develop the reputations of its excellent restaurants, cafés and food shops, and its Farmers' Market. The Cittaslow movement was seen as an exciting development along the trajectory established by success in

the 'Bloom' competitions, and it was consistent with Perth's ambitious goals for improving the quality of the environment, and developing its European credentials.

Cittaslow ('slow city', pronounced '*cheat-a-slow*') grew out of the Slow Food Movement founded in Italy in 1986. Cittaslow itself was established in 1999 by Carol Petrini and the mayors of four towns in northern Italy: Bra, Greve, Positano and Orvieto. It aims to improve the environment and quality of life in towns by slowing the pace of life, reducing pollution, litter and 'food miles', and by supporting local agriculture, businesses and community enterprises. The movement has expanded rapidly across the world, but retains a representative governing body, which still has its headquarters in Italy.

Towns seeking membership of the organisation are measured against 60 criteria and principles, which are the tangible benchmarks of the quality of life in a town or city. Among the factors assessed are many which are also associated with the 'Bloom' competitions, and others such as the availability of locally sourced food, support for local shops and businesses, provision of public transport, environmental protection, and a record of municipal action in relation to energy conservation, waste management and air pollution, etc.

A successful town will have achieved very good results in all these areas, and to ensure regular renewal of membership must show that it is striving for continuous improvement. Perth gained accreditation in March 2007, the first Cittaslow town in Scotland.

## Dynamic Small European City

Perth is anxious to portray itself as a dynamic small European City. The café culture, the 'Bloom' competitions and Cittaslow, are very much part of that outreach. But there is much more. Perth has strong twinning arrangements with four European cities. The connection with Aschaffenburg in Bavaria goes back to 1956, and is one of a group of twinning connections between Scottish and Bavarian cities. The twinning with Cognac is based on an obvious parallel involvement in distilling. That with Bydgoszcz in Poland was the result of a shared interest in the treatment of the blind, and the twinning with Pskov in western Russia arose from a partnership in a theatre production for young people. There are also twinning relationships with Perth in Ontario, Canada, Haikou in Hainan

Provost John Hulbert and Professor Miljenko Doric from Croatia, with the European flag, 2012.
© Angus Findlay.

Province in China, and Perth in Western Australia.

Through the various 'Friends' organisations, Perth's citizens work hard on these connections developing cultural, sporting, artistic, educational and business links, with several hundreds of individuals travelling between Perth and Europe on twinning visits each year.

## Europe Prize

Perth's focus on promoting the European Ideal was recognised by the Parliamentary Assembly of the Council of Europe in 2010 by the award of the European Diploma, and in 2011 by the Flag of Honour. These are the first two of four levels of the Europe Prize – The Diploma, The Flag of Honour, The Plaque of Honour, and finally The Prize itself. The Council of Europe was founded by the Treaty of London in 1949, to foster European co-operation through the promotion of human rights, democracy and the rule of law. The competition for the Europe Prize was established by its Parliamentary Assembly in 1955. Perth is blazing a European trail with this prize. Since the competition was set up there have been very few winners from the UK, and none from Scotland since 1995

Professor Miljenko Doric, who was a Member of the Croatian Parliament, and represented his country in the Council of Europe presented the Flag to the Provost at a ceremony in the Concert Hall.

## The Future for Perth

Perth's prominence in Scottish history has depended on its geopolitical position in the centre of the country, at an important crossing of the Tay, and at the gateway to the North. Its future as an important player among Scotland's cities and local authorities will depend on similar factors – especially its hub position in the transport network, and its newly recovered City Status. Together these should ensure that its economy thrives. Perth's people, its civic, arts and business organisations, and its local authority, have demonstrated an admirable ability to build on these strengths, to live according to the city's motto since 1976, '*Pro lege et libertate*' (for the Law and Liberty), and to develop those intangible qualities of political intuition and enterprise. These should serve it well in an uncertain future.

# Index

51st Highland Division 193, 205, 206
63 Tay Street (restaurant) 133

AK Bell Library 54, 58, 144, 145, 191, 210
Aberdeen Angus Cattle 134
*Aeneid* 58
Albert Close 32
Almondbank 33
An Seann Taigh (bar) 77
Anderson, Thomas 123, 124, 130
angling 183
Aschaffenburg 22, 43, 98, 215
Atholl Crescent 123, 125,126, 128, 170
Atholl Place 123, 125
Atholl Street 48, 78, 79, 123, 128, 130,
    131, 192, 193
Augustinian Abbey 156
Auld Hoose (bar) 77
Austin Reed 82
Aviva 54, 69, 188, 189, 211

bairn-rhymes (William Soutar) 44, 74
Balhousie Castle 23, 25, 54, 164–166
Ballathie 40
Bannockburn 34, 166
Barbour, John 33
Barnhill 148
Barossa, battle of 209
Barossa Place 130
Bartizan Belfry 92, 94
Battle of the Clans 164, 196, 197
Baxters Vennel 27, 55, 58, 81
Baxters' Incorporation 98, 213
Beaufort, Joan 124, 139, 140
Belhaven House 133
Bell, AK 52, 53, 165
Bell's Sports Centre 54, 165
Bell's Whisky 51, 52
bells 92–95, 153
Bellwood Nurseries 173
Bellwood Park 28, 151, 172–174, 179
Big Tree Country 161, 182
Binn Hill 180, 181
Bishop of Dunkeld 58, 174
Black Watch Association 23–25, 59, 60,
    107, 117, 217
Blackfriars 21, 116, 123, 124, 136
Blue Kinnoull 43, 180
Bowerswell 93, 152, 153, 154, 208, 210
Bothy, The (bar/restaurant) 120, 177
Branklyn Garden 179–181
Bridgend 52, 148, 154, 176
Broxden 42, 51, 191, 192
Buchan, John 43, 147
Bydgoszcz 22, 43, 198, 219

Café Breizh 71
Cairncross of Perth 83, 213

Cairncross, Alastair 87
Caithness Glass 176
Caledonian Road 147
Canal Street 32, 44, 55, 78, 79, 106, 107,
    108, 142, 169
Capital Asset (bar) 105
Carthusian Monastery 139, 175
Causeway 169, 170, 173, 177
Charlotte House 125
Charlotte Street 45, 121, 124, 125, 164, 197
Charterhouse Memorial 139
Cherrybank 182, 187, 188
Citadel 35, 72, 107, 140, 168
Cittaslow 18, 135, 201, 212, 218, 219
City Mills 31, 32, 122, 136, 137–139,
    197, 198
City Status 15, 18, 20, 21, 91, 160, 195, 220
city wall 17, 27, 29, 30–35, 55, 60, 63, 73,
    78, 101, 111, 115, 123, 136, 137, 139,
    145, 200
coat of arms 22, 43, 65, 71, 73, 88–91, 101,
    102, 113, 204, 213, 215, 216
Cognac 22, 43, 219
Concert Hall 24, 25, 41, 47, 54, 61, 97,
    111, 113–116, 118, 119, 197, 220
Connolly, James 72
Cordiners' Incorporation 98, 213
Council Chambers, New 68, 70, 90, 105
Council Chambers, Old 34, 63–67, 90, 105,
    198, 199
Cow Vennel 17, 77
Craigie Hill 182, 185, 188,189
Craigie Hill Golf Course 171, 172 182
Cream of the Well 43, 44
cricket 28, 53, 164, 195
Crieff Road 33, 187, 192, 194, 195
Cromwell 35, 72, 107, 140, 168
Cunningham-Graham Close 62
Curfew Row 116
curling 25, 108, 159, 164, 189–191
Cutlog Vennel 119

Deans @ Let's Eat (restaurant) 131
Deuchar, A.S. 58, 59, 75, 202
Deuchny Woods 180, 181
Dewar, John (Lord Forteviot) 48–50
Dewar, Thomas (Lord Dewar of Homestall)
    49, 50
Dewar's Centre 189–191
Dickens (bar) 78
District Court 64, 105
Dominican Friary 31, 123
Doo'cot Park 53
Douglas, David 43, 161, 162
Douglas, Gavin 58, 174
Dry Arch 33, 36, 37, 40, 42, 43, 45, 46
Dunkeld Road 32, 193–195, 203

Eagle of Perth 45
Edinburgh Road 75, 102, 133, 135, 166–
    168, 185, 187
Edrington Distillers 48, 50, 51, 149, 191, 192
Eneados o Virgil 58
Europe Prize 212, 220

Fair Maid's House 25, 116–118, 196, 197,
    213, 214
Famous Grouse 50–52, 120, 129, 149,
    191, 192
Famous Grouse statue 192
Farmers' Market 24, 199–203, 218
Fergusson Gallery 25, 45, 103, 108, 109,
    110, 132, 133, 142, 168
Fergusson, JD 25, 108, 109, 110, 114
Fiscal's house 75, 106
fishing 33, 183
Flemish Candelabrum 88, 89
Fleshers Vennel 27, 72, 76, 77
Fleshers' Incorporation 77, 99, 213
flooding 17, 19, 21, 26, 31, 32, 35–38,
    40–47, 164, 166, 167, 169, 171, 178–
    180, 192, 206, 208, 213
Fountain Close 58, 75,
Friarton Bridge 28, 39, 149, 181, 184

Gaelic 19, 28, 77, 146, 156
Gannochy Trust 51, 53, 54, 114, 141, 145,
    165, 173
Geddes, Sir Patrick 173, 177
General Accident 68, 69, 179, 189
George Duncan Athletics Arena 194
George Street 32, 60, 63, 70, 71, 100
Gillian Forbes 22, 43, 74
Gillies of Perth 61, 62,
Glasgow Road 187, 188,
Gloag, Matthew 48, 50, 120,
Glover, Catharine 116, 197, 199
Glover, Simon 116, 197, 199
Glovers' Incorporation 43, 60, 66, 98, 213
Goldeneye 44
Goosander 106
Gowrie Conspiracy 56, 107, 156, 175
Gowrie, Earl of 56, 107, 140, 156, 158, 175
Gowrie House 56, 58, 106, 107
Graham, Sir Thomas (See Baron Lynedoch)
Granary, The 137, 138
Gravestones 20, 107, 108, 153, 176
Gray, Effie 152, 177
Gray, George 152, 155
Gray, Melville 93, 153
Greyfriars Cemetery 10, 107, 108, 169
Greyfriars Friary 31, 107
Greyfriars Quay 31, 32, 55
Guildhall 72, 73, 213
Guildry Incorporation 72, 98, 213, 214, 216

Hal o' the Wynd 122, 139, 197–199
Halkerston Tower 87, 88
Hammermen's Incorporation 66, 88, 99, 113
Hay, Sir George (See Earl of Kinnoull)
Heather Garden 173, 174
Heiton architects 64, 65, 72, 100, 103, 105,106, 143, 144, 150
High Street 18, 19, 27, 31, 37, 55–57, 59–64, 68, 70–73, 75, 78, 79, 81, 90, 97, 98, 100, 103, 105, 113, 114, 118, 119, 121, 136, 137, 198, 199, 200
Highland Distillers 50
Highland Fault 19
Highland House 193
Horners Lane 17, 77
Horsecross 114, 119
Hospital Street 139
Huntingtower Hotel 31, 33

Isabella, Countess of Buchan 128
Isla Road 148

Jamieson's Buildings 131
Jeanfield & District Lads 211
Jeanfield Cemetery 67, 210
Jeanfield Road 191, 210, 211

Karnival Klub (Night club) 120, 121
Kincarrathie Quarry 157
Kincarrathie House 53, 54
Kinfauns 50, 51, 107, 120, 149, 181
King Charles I 175, 213
King Charles II 159, 214
King David I 137
King David II 34
King Edward Street 62, 70, 73, 75, 77, 78, 81, 97, 98, 204, 215
King Edward VII Memorial 72, 98, 99, 204
King George VI 24, 67, 113
King James I 21, 116, 124, 139, 140
King James IV 85, 170
King James V 174
King James VI 37, 56, 127, 139–142, 145, 156, 161, 170, 175,
King James Place 132
King James VI Golf Club 170, 171
King James VI Golf Course 39, 171
King James VI Hospital 139
King Jimmy's Cider 171
King Kenneth MacAlpin 156
King Robert the Bruce 34, 66, 84, 127, 128, 157
King Robert II 138
King Robert III 28, 164, 166, 197, 198, 199
King Street 129, 132, 135, 139, 199
Kings Arms Close 62
Kings Place 132
Kinnoull Aisle 153, 172, 173, 174, 175, 177
Kinnoull, Earl of 38, 56, 132, 164, 165, 175
Kinnoull's Lodging House 56, 57, 61
Kinnoull Folly 29, 181
Kinnoull Hill 28, 29, 38, 50, 51, 103, 106,

127, 130, 149–151, 173, 174, 177, 178, 180, 181
Kinnoull Parish Church 152–154, 210
Kinnoull school 58
Kinnoull Street 62, 75, 78, 79, 98, 118–121, 131
Kinnoull Village 148
Kirk Vennels 27, 61, 76, 81
Kirkgate 31, 60, 61, 71–73
Kirking of the Council 212, 216, 217
Knox, John 21, 30, 85–87, 93, 147, 151

Lade 17, 30, 31–34, 47, 60, 63, 75, 104, 111, 124, 136–139, 192, 194
Lakeland 75, 82
Library Lodge 146
Lochie Brae 187
Lockit Book 214
Lodge Scoon 126
Log Boat 19
Lord Gray of Kinfauns 181
Lord John Murray's House 25, 116, 117, 197
Lord Lieutenant 205, 216, 217
Lorimer, Sir Robert 86, 87, 89, 96, 97, 204, 205
Low's Work 31, 33
Lynedoch, Baron (Sir Thomas Graham). 130, 208, 209
Lynedoch Monument 38, 46, 164, 208

Mailer Hill 29, 182
Mansfield, Earl of 156 - 160, 190
Mansfield Mausoleum 156, 157, 158, 160
Market (Mercat) Cross 31, 61, 71, 72, 98, 160, 16
Marshall Monument 111–113, 123
Marshall Place 22, 39, 123, 132, 133, 135, 166, 199
Marshall, Thomas Hay 112, 123, 124, 128–130, 164, 199
Masonic Lodge 124, 126, 127, 128, 211
McDiarmid Park 195
McEwen, John 146
McEwens of Perth 82
MacNab, John 43, 147
Meal Vennel 27, 31, 62
Meconopsis (See Blue Kinnoull)
Melville Street 72, 97, 130, 210
Memorial garden 35, 45, 46, 206
Mercers of Aldie 71
Mercure Hotel 138
Methven Street (North & South) 32, 34, 75, 77–79, 121, 122, 131, 136, 137, 197, 198, 202, 203
Middle Free Church (See Red Church)
Mill Street 31, 32, 75, 79, 111, 118–123, 138, 197
Mill Wynd 139, 196, 197, 198
Millais, Sir John Everett 114, 152–155, 173, 177
Monart glass 176
Moncreiffe Hill 182, 183

Moncreiffe Island 28, 38, 109, 169, 184
Monk, Carthusian 127
Monk, General 35
Monk's tower 31, 35, 44
Moot Hill 149, 155–157, 159, 160
Morris, Margaret 25, 109, 110
Mousetrap 43, 147
Muirton 41, 47, 164, 192, 194
Murray, David 60
Murray, Sir David (See Mansfield, Earl of)
Murray, Lord George 117
Murray, James (See Murray Royal Hospital)
Murray, Lord John (See Lord John Murray's House)
Murray Royal Hospital 149, 150, 154
Murray Star Maze 160
Museum & Art Gallery 21, 23–25, 35, 41, 59, 60, 111–115, 123, 137, 142, 153, 209
Museum of Racing 163

Necessity Brae 187–189
Needless Road 187
Norie-Miller, Sir Francis 68, 69
Norie-Miller Park 28, 69, 173, 178, 179
Norie-Miller, Sir Stanley 69, 178, 179
North Boat Vennel 55
North Church 75, 121, 122
North Inch 23, 25, 28, 33, 35, 37, 38, 42, 45–47, 123–125, 128, 129, 131, 162, 164, 165, 170–172, 183, 185, 194–197, 206
North Inch Campus 194
North Inch Golf Course 171
North Korean War Memorial 211
North Port 116, 124, 125, 197

Old Academy 129, 130
Old High Street 136, 137, 198, 200, 211
Old Ship Inn 60, 61
Oliphants Vennel 27, 55, 82
Organ, St John's Kirk 96
Organ, St Ninian's Cathedral 132

Parklands Hotel 135
Pearls 83
Peregrine falcon 106
Perth & District Pipe Band 90, 164, 202, 215, 216
Perth Academy 109, 121, 177
Perth Artisan Golf Club 170, 171
Perth Bridge 33, 36, 37, 39, 43–46, 101–103, 111, 113, 123, 124, 148, 164, 172, 179, 182
Perth Castle 35, 46
Perth College (UHI) 194, 195
Perth Festival of the Arts 24, 115
Perth Grammar School 76, 194
Perth Highland Games 51, 164
Perth in Bloom 218
Perth Leisure Pool 50, 189
Perth, Ontario, Canada 23, 90, 217, 219
Perth Racecourse 149, 160, 161, 163

Perth Royal Infirmary 145, 191, 192
Perth's Prisons 63, 88, 185
Perth Show 51, 168
Perth Tennis Club 165
Perth Theatre 14, 54, 75, 119
Perth Waterworks (See Fergusson gallery)
Perth Working Men's Garden Association 170
Perthshire Society of Natural Science 107, 112
Pig'Halle (restaurant) 75
Pillar Sculptures 19, 22, 43, 35, 42, 43, 44,
    74, 83, 90, 147, 162, 178, 180, 205, 213
Pillory, The 63
Pinetum 160, 161
Pitcullen Crescent 148
Pitheavlis Castle 187, 188
Pitheavlis Estate 68, 69, 189
Playhouse 122
Police Station 32, 192, 193
Polish Army 67, 210
Polish War Memorial 210
Post Office 111
*Prince Albert* (sculpture) 125
Prince Charles Edward Stuart 62, 72, 188
Prince Charles, Duke of Rothesay 24, 159,
    160, 202, 203, 214
Princes Street 75, 76, 97, 133, 194, 200
promontory 18, 19, 26, 28, 36, 42, 43, 81,
    216, 217
Provost's Badge 212
Provost's Street Lamp 126
Pskov 22, 43, 219
Pullar Buildings 118, 119, 211
Pullars of Perth 66, 111, 118, 119, 153

Quarrymill 36, 53, 182
Queen Victoria 49, 66, 67, 101, 102, 143,
    144, 159, 190, 214
Queen's Bridge 39, 41, 42, 44, 173, 178

Railway Bridge 20, 28, 38, 39, 42, 108,
    132, 135, 171, 172, 173, 184
Railway Station 39, 101, 135, 142, 143, 188
Railway Viaduct 39, 134, 135
Red Brig 31, 32, 47, 60, 61, 63, 111
Red Church 64, 103–105
Reformation 21, 30, 81, 85, 93, 94, 95,
    104, 131, 139, 140, 151, 156, 174
Reid, Robert 123, 129, 133, 185
Remembrance Day 204, 205, 210, 216, 217
*Return of the Prodigal* sculpture 189
River Almond 31, 33, 40, 47, 192
River Garry 40, 41
River Isla 40
River Tay 17–21, 26, 28, 29, 32, 33, 35, 36,
    38, 40, 41, 42, 50, 83. 109, 111, 127,
    148, 154, 156, 169, 178, 183, 220
*River Tay Themes* 46
River Tummel 40, 41
Riverside Park 172–174
Robertson Trust 50
Rodney Gardens 28, 172, 177, 178
Roman Bridge 38

Ropemakers Close 27
Rose Anderson 130
Rose Terrace 123, 128, 129, 130, 164
Rotary Clock 62
Roy's Military Map 185, 187
Royal Burgh (Perth) 20, 21, 23, 51, 63, 66,
    89–91, 118, 177, 213, 216
Royal Burgh (Scone) 156, 160
Royal Charter 20, 21, 35, 39, 91, 159, 160,
    195, 218
Royal George Hotel 101–104
Royal National Lifeboat Institution 54
Royal Perth Golfing Society 125, 170
Royal Scottish Geographical Society 24–26,
    117, 197
Ruskin, John 152
Ruthven, William & John (see Gowrie, Earl
    of) Ruthvenfield 31, 33

salmon fishing 33, 137, 183
Salmon Run 44
Salutation hotel 59, 60, 75
Salvation Army 61, 77
Sandeman, Sir Archibald 120, 145
Sandeman (Bar/restaurant) 120, 121
Scone (Abbey, Palace, Village) 33–35, 56,
    126–128, 137, 149, 156–162, 174, 182,
    190, 214
Scots Language Resource Centre 146
Scots Language Society 58
Scott Street 73, 78, 79, 132, 203
Scott, Sir Walter 18, 49, 66, 133, 135, 196,
    198, 199, 218
Scottish Crown 83, 128
Sculpture Trail 173, 175
Season Time and Place Sculpture. 129, 130
Sharp's Educational Institute 121
Sheriff Court House 44, 56, 75, 103, 106
Shetland Pony Stud Book 147
Simon, David 30, 31
Skate Park 168
Skinnergate 27, 31, 55, 60–63, 70, 71, 100
Smeaton, John 19, 36, 37, 38, 40
Society of High Constables 88, 205, 214–216
Soutar Ring 73
Soutar, William 43, 44, 73, 74, 145, 208
South Inch 22, 28, 29, 35, 42, 45, 75, 77,
    79, 103, 107, 108, 123, 132–135, 140,
    142, 162, 164, 166 - 168, 170, 185, 199
South Port 185, 187
South Street 27, 31, 39, 55, 58, 62, 63, 72,
    75–79, 81, 97, 105, 106, 136, 139, 185,
    200, 202, 213
Spectraglass 176
Spey Tower 31
Speygate 31, 55, 63
St Anns Lane 76
St Catherines retail park 32, 193, 203
St John Street 59, 75, 78, 81, 82, 83, 213
St John the Baptist Episcopalian Church 97
St John the Baptist Roman Catholic Church
    72, 97, 210

St John's Academy 194
St John's Kirk 19, 21, 23, 27, 28, 30, 31,
    54, 55, 60, 71, 76, 78, 81, 84–88, 95,
    96, 115, 137, 140, 141, 151,153, 158,
    182, 204, 205, 208, 209, 216
St John's Centre 62, 75, 77, 80, 98, 203, 204
St Johnstone Football Club 90, 195
St Leonard's Bank 135, 166
St Leonard's Church (former) 142
St Leonard's-in-the-Fields Church 133–135
St Leonard's Priory 135
St Martyn 98
St Mary's Chapel 64, 140
St Mary's Monastery 149, 150, 151, 152, 174
St Matthew's Church 104, 105, 173
St Ninian's Cathedral 24, 31, 115, 131,
    132, 151
St Paul's Church 136, 137
Stanners Island 37
Station Hotel 142, 144
Stone of Destiny 128, 155–157

Tailors' Incorporation 58, 99, 213
Tay Descent 26
Tay Street 17–22, 26, 35, 38, 39, 42, 44,
    45, 55, 56, 63, 64, 65, 68, 70, 74, 75,
    83, 100, 102–109, 112, 115, 132, 135,
    147, 162, 173, 178, 179, 180, 185, 191,
    202, 213, 216
tayberry 43
tennis 124, 165
Theatre Royal 131
Tolbooth 31, 63, 64
*Torse de Femme* (statue) 109
Town clock 95
Trinity Church of the Nazarene 145
Turret Port 31, 136

Unthank 42

Vasart glass 176
Victoria Bridge 39
Virgil 58

walled garden 151
Water Vennel 55
Watergate 27, 31, 55, 56, 57, 58, 60, 63,
    68, 70, 71, 81, 100, 213
*Wave* (sculpture) 146
Weavers' Incorporation 98, 213
Wellshill cemetery 67, 210, 211
Whisky 17, 22, 48–52, 191
White Stuff, The 82
Willowgate Trout Fisheries 28, 184
Wilson Street 74
Wrights' Incorporation 58, 60, 89

York Place 145, 146, 146, 200
Young (architects) 68, 103, 106, 107, 147
Ysart, Paul 175, 176

# **Luath** Press Limited

*committed to publishing well written books worth reading*

LUATH PRESS takes its name from Robert Burns, whose little collie Luath (*Gael.,* swift or nimble) tripped up Jean Armour at a wedding and gave him the chance to speak to the woman who was to be his wife and the abiding love of his life. Burns called one of 'The Twa Dogs' Luath after Cuchullin's hunting dog in Ossian's *Fingal*. Luath Press was established in 1981 in the heart of Burns country, and now resides a few steps up the road from Burns' first lodgings on Edinburgh's Royal Mile. Luath offers you distinctive writing with a hint of unexpected pleasures.

Most bookshops in the UK, the US, Canada, Australia, New Zealand and parts of Europe either carry our books in stock or can order them for you. To order direct from us, please send a £sterling cheque, postal order, international money order or your credit card details (number, address of cardholder and expiry date) to us at the address below. Please add post and packing as follows: UK – £1.00 per delivery address; overseas surface mail – £2.50 per delivery address; overseas airmail – £3.50 for the first book to each delivery address, plus £1.00 for each additional book by airmail to the same address. If your order is a gift, we will happily enclose your card or message at no extra charge.

**Luath** Press Limited
543/2 Castlehill
The Royal Mile
Edinburgh EH1 2ND
Scotland
Telephone: 0131 225 4326 (24 hours)
email: sales@luath.co.uk
Website: www.luath.co.uk